A WORLD WITHOUT IDENTITY

Also by Patrick Paul Garlinger

When Thought Turns to Light
Seeds of Light
Bending Time

A WORLD WITHOUT IDENTITY

THE SACRED TASK OF UNITING HUMANITY

Patrick Paul Garlinger

Anastasis Books
New York, New York

Paperback ISBN: 978-0-9985563-4-5
E-book ISBN: 978-0-9985563-5-2
Library of Congress Control Number: 2019913448

Cover and book design by Colin Rolfe
Distributed by Epigraph Publishing Service

Anastasis Books
New York, New York
www.anastasisbooks.com

CONTENTS

PREFACE

*T*his is a book about spirituality and social change. It is also, importantly, a *channeled* text. For readers unfamiliar with channeling, the term refers to the receipt of information, words, and images from a source outside of a person's mind, usually from a higher authority. An example of a well-known channel is Esther Hicks, who channels an entity known as Abraham; together, Abraham-Hicks, as they are called in the singular, popularized a concept known as the Law of Attraction, which holds that you are manifesting your life according to the energy of your thoughts and where you focus them. One of the most influential spiritual works of our time, *A Course in Miracles*, is also a channeled work. Although Marianne Williamson is well known for disseminating the messages of *ACIM*, it was Helen Schucman who first downloaded the material that became the book. In fact, there are many individuals who identify themselves as channels for higher beings, and for the vast majority, their stated purpose is to help humanity grow and experience a higher state of consciousness.

For a lot of people, however, the very idea of channeling is a bridge too far, or an instant red flag. You either don't believe that channeled writing exists, and therefore this is just some sophisticated cover or subterfuge to claim a higher authority for its persuasive value, or you grant that my experience may seem real to me, but it should be examined as a basis for mental illness. Because people have no framework or personal experience of their own to draw on when it comes to channeling, and because so many false prophets have claimed to speak for a higher authority, many people's normal response is to reject any claims of access to channeling or psychic intuition.

I understand that perspective, as I was once a disbeliever of all things related to religion and spirituality.

Until I experienced it myself, I never entertained the notion of being a channel, even though I had seen and read other channeled works. Channeling began for me in the midst of a profound spiritual awakening that forever altered the course of my life. Near the end of a three-year apprenticeship with my spiritual teacher, I experienced what is traditionally known as a *kundalini* awakening. In the Hindu tradition, kundalini is the dormant spiritual energy at the base of the spine. When it awakens, it travels up through a passageway known as the *sushumna*, which runs up the spinal column to the crown of the head, through each of the chakras.

A kundalini awakening is an intense experience. For nearly six months, I spent hours each day as the kundalini coursed up and down the sushumna, opening and cleansing each of my chakras. At times it was utterly blissful; at others it was exhausting. One month into this process, I heard a voice—a very powerful, authoritative, and loving voice—that simply said, "We are going to write, and we are going to write quickly." This voice identified itself simply as "the Council of Light"—a collective of Light Beings who help to oversee the evolution of humanity. Within days, I began to channel. As the Council had forewarned, the words came quickly, and I typed frantically, barely able to keep up with the "transmissions," as they called them. As the transmissions came down, I felt gentle raindrops of energy on the crown of my head. At times the energy was so overwhelming I would lose the thread and fall into a deep state of bliss.

One question I am often asked is whether channeling is the same as automatic writing. As a former lawyer and professor, I'm quite familiar with automatic writing. When I get into that kind of state, what one might call "flow," the words simply pour out onto the page, unencumbered by self-doubt. The usual fits and starts of conjuring decent prose are absent. The right choice of verbs, the perfect sentence structure, the clever analogy or metaphor are all automatic. It's my voice, at its best and with the least amount of effort.

Channeling is a different experience. Whereas automatic writing feels like the words emanate from me, channeled writing feels very much like material that emanates from a different source. The voice I hear—the voice of the Council—as the words come through me is not the one I usually experience in my head. The voice of the Council sounds more authoritative, deeper, and quite loving, if pointed and direct. The style of the language and prose, while borrowing from my idiosyncrasies, is not my style, which tends to be more flowery. (The reader is welcome to compare my prose style from *When Thought Turns to Light*, my first book of spiritual writing, with this work and its predecessors.)

In addition to the feeling, the content is never intentional. On the occasions that my writing has been automatic, I sat down to write on a particular issue or address a certain topic only to discover that my mind had already worked out what to say, and the words poured out onto the page. With channeling, however, I have always been struck by the unanticipated directions the Council would take, and for that reason, the transmissions never followed a linear, logical fashion. In contrast with automatic writing, I haven't always agreed with their messages, and in the text I therefore pose questions, set in italics, in direct response to the transmissions. Finally, whereas automatic writing feels like a smooth and seamless process, channeling is always accompanied by an intense rush of energy; it happens in short bursts, and often leaves me in a blissful, thoughtless state—the kind of state that people often hope to achieve in meditation, but rarely do.

There is, however, little I can do to persuade you of the veracity of my experience. That is true, of course, of all experience. You will never know how I experience sadness, fear, anger, or any other emotion. You will always be working with your own experience and the translation that occurs as we communicate in words. By way of example, no one can really claim that what they experience as love feels the same as what someone else claims to experience as love. There are many experiences that others have had that you haven't, and you cannot validate or invalidate that other person's experience. Can you imagine men telling women what they must have experienced during childbirth? As far as I am aware, no man has ever given birth, and while he can witness it, he cannot experience it. Something similar may be said of channeling.

This may sound like an extended defense of channeling, but it is not. Rather, consider this a lengthy call to ask you to suspend your judgment and disbelief and evaluate these words without needing to validate or invalidate them based on their origin. Instead, evaluate their persuasive authority as you would any other person's writing, were it produced by the internal firings of the brain's neurons and synapses. (I can assure you, mine were also involved in this process.) In other words, assume, if it is easier for you, that these words were not channeled, but my own mind's creation, and then ask yourself if you are persuaded based on the normal standards of logic and persuasion that would guide any other argument you might analyze.

For even if you do not subscribe to the origin of this work, you can still believe its messages and find value in its wisdom.

❄

My first channeled work, *Seeds of Light*, was transmitted to me in March and April of 2016. The second volume, *Bending Time*, also took about two months to receive. Like its predecessors, this book was transmitted to me in roughly two months' time, beginning in August that same year, shortly after the transmissions of *Bending Time* were finished. In short, the entire trilogy of channeled works was produced in just over seven months. The amount of time that transpired between transmission and publication of this book, as I was editing the manuscript, meant that I had time to receive some additional transmissions in early 2019 to bring the book up to date.

A World Without Identity is the culmination of the messages of its two older siblings. *Seeds of Light* focused on our understanding of the self and the nature of human consciousness. It argued that the vast majority of us are creatures of mass or collective consciousness. We perceive the world as a potential threat and reduce it to convenient binaries so that we can evaluate whether it is good or bad for us. Our purpose for being here as humans, though, is to learn that we are not separate from the Divine, and that we can awaken to the Christ Consciousness—a state of mind beyond judgment in which we see the world as it truly is and with eyes of unconditional love.

Bending Time looked at how our collective consciousness has shaped and distorted our relationships with each other, with a particular emphasis on how we relate to time itself. That volume stressed that we do not see each other in the present moment, but through the eyes of the past, and accompanied by our previous experiences. As a result, we don't actual encounter the world as it truly is in the now. This is especially true of our interpersonal relationships, in which we see each other as partial, limited versions, based on our prior encounters with other people. As we embrace the Christ Consciousness, however, we can learn to "bend" time by allowing for all possibilities to come forth and emerge in the present. In that way, we can experience the "fullness" of another person rather than blocking their full potential.

This third work demonstrates how this collective consciousness rooted in separation has created our political, economic, legal, and social systems, and how the Christ Consciousness can engage those systems to create real transformation—a point that is elaborated on in more detail in my (non-channeled) introduction to this volume.

In preparing this work for publication, I have endeavored to strike a balance between the order of the original transmissions and the reader's need for linearity, logic, and readability. I have endeavored, as best as I can, to respect the unique style and energy of the words that came through while also editing it for intelligibility. The result is, I hope, sufficiently faithful to the original transmission yet more accessible to the reader.

Nevertheless, I have also accepted that part of this trilogy's approach is to make linearity less important, and to ask the reader to trust the journey. That may make for a different reading experience. In that regard, I recommend reading a chapter or two and letting the material sink in, then continuing with a few more installments. This is not a book to be devoured in one sitting. At first it might seem like the chapters jump from topic to topic. You may even wish for the book to weave the chapters together. But the Council eschews this approach, leaving you to make the necessary connections.

You may need to go back over certain passages, particularly as connections between earlier and later chapters become apparent to you. Over time you will see that a different kind of logic shapes the book's structure as it moves from material about our inner world and how our minds are built on separation to different aspects of our society and how those aspects are built on separation. The chapters thus subtly move back and forth between the individual to society, intertwining these two dimensions and guiding the reader to adopt a new perspective on how to be a part of society.

Treat the book like a journey; you don't know where you'll end up, and you are going to take some odd twists and turns. How you read and relate to this book is itself a model of the way our logical minds need to relate to life itself. Reading the book, then, is its own form of spiritual practice. Trust that it is taking you where you need to go.

Patrick Paul Garlinger
New York, New York
March 2019

INTRODUCTION

Most people look at the world and think it needs to be changed. They see a planet rife with political corruption and dysfunction, ravaged by environmental disaster and climate change, and torn apart by economic disparity, prejudice, and injustice. Many books have tackled the need for social and political change, with in-depth diagnoses of the problems that plague our political, economic, legal, and social systems. Few of those books would be catalogued as spiritual writing.

Most spiritual books limit their insights to the individual or relationships. They offer insights about the meaning of life and provide tools or inspiration for living with greater purpose and meaning. To the extent that spiritual works have a broader goal of reshaping the world, they operate on the assumption that as people change, the world will change as well. And while it is true that an authentic and radical transformation of our society cannot happen without inner spiritual transformation, the link between the individual and society demands a more direct treatment.

The main thesis of *A World Without Identity* is that our society's structures and systems are a reflection of our minds' collective belief that we are separate from each other. Separation is the fundamental belief that we are single, autonomous individuals, unique from each other in time and space. *I am me and not you, right now. And in the next second, I am still me and you are still you, and I am still not you, and vice versa.* This is our everyday perception of life on the planet. By virtue of being separate and autonomous, each of us is potentially vulnerable to harm by another. My existence does not depend on your existence, and therefore if you cease to exist, I will still exist. This very notion of separation sets up a tension between each and every person.

But how to evaluate whether someone is a threat? Our minds seek ways of deciding what is safe and what is not, and it thus looks for difference. In this regard, people and objects are not just separate from me—they are *different* from me in a variety of ways. To the ego, differences create tension and fear, for those differences may be a threat, whereas sameness breeds a sense of familiarity and safety. The fundamental consequence is that most people are driven by self-interest and survival based on their assessment of difference and sameness, of drawing arbitrary lines that the mind uses to interpret whether you are safe or in danger. When we start seeing others as threats to our own survival, we stop seeing each other as divine beings, as "Seeds of Light" (the Council's term for our divinity and connection to God).[1]

By contrast, *oneness* is the spiritual principle that we are all interconnected and interdependent. We do not live in isolation or complete autonomy, as if we could just ignore each other or cut each other entirely out of our lives. Even if we tried, we would find it impossible; virtually every aspect of our lives depends on someone else's contribution, whether it is through food, employment, transportation, health care, etc.

Oneness has gained a lot of traction in spiritual circles in recent years as people recognize that our common humanity is far greater than our perceived differences. When you engage in spiritual practices such as meditation, prayer, and energy work, or have experiences in higher consciousness (sometimes aided by plant medicine or psychedelics), you may experience that sense of unity and the incredible bliss that accompanies it. Many people emerge from these states with a deep conviction that, in fact, we are all one and connected in ways that our conventional minds fail to grasp. For the Council, that state of unity is known as the Christ Consciousness—a state of complete and total unconditional love and acceptance of all that is.

Yet for many of us, even after such experiences, our spiritual energy evaporates when we get up from the meditation cushion, leave the church or temple, or the blissful effects of an ingested substance wear off. Once we're back in the "real world," our normal ways of relating to life return to the surface. At best, we're lucky to embrace love, gratitude, equanimity, and compassion when we're talking about ourselves, our families, and our friends. But when we're talking about our politicians? Wall Street? Lawyers and judges? Elections? Hardly ever. This is because we either haven't practiced bringing that mindset to the world of politics (and spiritual traditions have often failed to explain how to relate spiritually to the world at large), or we believe that these qualities won't really work in that arena, and that we need to fight and conquer the opposition to create a better government and world.

Bringing a spiritual perspective to our political, financial, and legal systems is a daunting task. Our political realm is extremely polarized, and our exchanges on social media reflect enormous divisions of opinion. When we engage with broader questions and social issues likes economic inequality, political partisanship, fair elections, judicial activism, mass incarceration, or white privilege, we very quickly fall back into the throes of the ego and its basic separation-rooted responses.

Even those of us who have cultivated feelings of connection, peace, and equanimity through spiritual practices often relinquish that mindset when engaging with these thorny topics. The task is made all the more difficult by the many members of the public who don't have any spiritual connection at all, and who routinely resort to name-calling, trolling, and other divisive means of engagement. As a result, the language of our everyday interactions, primarily through social media, displays all of the negative aspects of our egos, including judgment, discrimination, and emotional reactivity.

The message of this book is that our normal methods of engaging these domains and creating change end up replicating the very structure of separation that has already produced a divided and unequal society. Indeed, our engagement with these areas is nearly always marked by criticism, blame, and division. We split the world into binaries like rich and poor, progressives and conservatives, whites and non-whites, to name a few, and then we have to pick sides, with one side being "right" and the other side being "wrong" or carrying the blame. The changes that are made are usually "hard-fought" compromises between two opposing factions. Change is piecemeal, incremental, and often subject to being undone after shifts in power between our two main political parties.

Furthermore, it can often feel like we are powerless to effect much change in the face of the enormous resources and power that have been concentrated in the hands of a few individuals and corporations. We might even feel that as normal, everyday citizens, we don't have much of a role to play in creating change or sufficient power to make meaningful contributions. That sense of powerlessness is one of the reasons so few people vote in elections.

But that does not mean we *are* powerless. To the contrary, the book's message is that if we want to transform our society, we must engage each of these realms with the same kind of love and compassion that we bring to ourselves and to our relationships when we are on a spiritual path. In that regard, the Council's message is that our relationship to this broader sphere is no different than our relationship to any other single person. We must enter those domains with the same level of intentionality, compassion, and love that we use when we seek to heal an interpersonal relationship. With every action we take, we infuse our collective system with a certain level of energy. We must retrain ourselves to relate to the broader society from a place of unconditional love. This is not, to be sure, the normal path to social and political change, which usually emphasizes plans and ideas for reform, calls to make those changes infused with combative or unifying rhetoric ("fighting for our rights," "yes, we can," or "make America great again"), and the inevitable squabbling, finger-pointing, and compromises that are the hallmarks of our political system. But this change in approach is necessary if we as humans are going to move forward and create a united world.

Rarely does the Council offer much in the way of prescriptive advice on particular topics. Nevertheless, it tackles a few social issues that may be controversial for some readers, principally abortion and reparations to African Americans. With respect to abortion, for example, they are adamant that neither the pro-life nor pro-choice position is accurate. For them, life begins at the moment the embryo is fertilized and the cells start replicating and dividing. They are unequivocal about this fact, but are equally clear that the woman always has the right to exercise her free will, and thus abortion is not a "sin." With respect to reparations, the Council is equally clear that the trauma that was inflicted on blacks in our country, and which continues to this day through rampant discrimination and systemic inequality, must be dealt with collectively. Reparations are necessary for us to confront the legacy of slavery and ongoing mistreatment of African Americans.

Otherwise, the book refuses to provide a detailed set of instructions for how we reform and transform our society or our systems of government, finance, law, etc. It may be disappointing for some readers to hear that, according to the Council, providing us with a new model for our world would short-circuit the path that we must follow to get there. I can sympathize with those readers. But the Council's point is that, from our current perspective, as highly unenlightened people, an enlightened world would not make sense to us or, frankly, even be *visible* to us. We wouldn't see or perceive the world as enlightened, because our perceptions shape how reality appears to us, and our perceptions are not enlightened. It would be like saying to someone who has never seen a particular color—let's call it "sea-green-gerine"—that an enlightened world looks "sea-green-gerine," so now imagine what that world looks like. You would hear this description, and it would be meaningless to you. You would have no idea what it looked like. In other words, unless you have traveled the path to get there, you wouldn't recognize the destination even if you had a picture and a map to lead you there.

In that regard, the Council points out that the path *is* the destination, and that if we knew where we were going, we would try to do all sorts of things to speed things up, take short cuts, etc., only to find that we had recreated another version our current world rather than an enlightened world.

For the Council, the path or blueprint is *how* we relate to these realms, not *what* is created at the end of some seemingly linear sequence of events or actions taken that we *think* will result in unity. Altering our systems of government, finance, education, justice, etc., does not require that we dismantle them in one fell swoop and erect a new system. We can't just sit down and redesign everything from the ground up and then execute it, as if that would create unity. The point of these messages is that it is the *intention* and *energy* that we bring to our actions which determines how we will reshape our world. We must always be looking toward inclusiveness and unity—moving toward oneness—by fostering it internally and then bringing it to all of our external interactions. Because, in truth, there is no difference between our internal states and the external world.

It is hard to deny that most people do not know how to engage with our political, legal, and financial systems without judgment, blame, condemnation, and pessimism. It is equally hard to deny the gridlock, partisanship, and corruption that mark our current political system. As a result, the book leads the reader through various aspects of our society, showing how they reflect our fundamental consciousness of separation, and invites the reader to adopt a new perspective and a new way of relating to that aspect of our world. Our engagement with our political, economic, and legal systems must be based on a sincere intention for us to move into collective unity. For the Council, it is critical that we see and treat each interaction with our society as capable of accomplishing that unity.

That doesn't mean there are not obvious ways to reform our systems that we already know of but haven't yet enacted (i.e., ending mass incarceration or economic inequality). But the Council isn't interested in telling us, for example, precisely how our criminal justice system or government should be changed. Rather, we must ourselves move toward those reforms, remaining vigilant against ways we might fall back into separation. As the reader will learn, it matters less *what* we envision for ourselves than *how* we go about it—operating always with the intention that everyone, including those who seem opposed to reform and transformation, be included in a new world.

We also have to abandon our usual metrics and time horizons for change. All too often, we are wedded to the idea that an election—particularly the election of our nation's president—will usher in a wholesale and radical transformation of our political system. We cast a vote thinking that one person's installment as the executive of our country will be enough. Then, when changes do not appear to happen, we become despondent and cynical, and we resort to blame, judgment, and dismissal. But the Council is clear here too: We cannot expect changes to happen that quickly, or *even in our lifetime*. The horizon for change is much longer, and therefore it is the intention with which we cast our votes, or engage in any way with our systems of governance, that matters. In sum, it is more important that you cast your vote with the intention of uniting humanity than with the intention that your candidate win.

Finally, a few words about the title are warranted. The book's title is meant to be provocative. A reader might initially assume that this is a clarion call to abandon our individual identities in the name of some idealized commonality or conformity. This would miss the mark. Any call to flatten ourselves, denude ourselves of what makes us unique, and somehow embrace conformity would be the demand of an ego that cannot tolerate difference. To the contrary, the truest exaltation of difference comes from not requiring the self to be any one thing.

Nevertheless, the Council repeatedly speaks about the limits of identity, as we understand it and have constructed it.[2] We need a new model of identity, a new understanding of the self. Presently, our identities tend to reduce the complexity of our world to discrete and overly simplified categories, and in so doing suppress the diversity that lies within each one of us. In truth, each of us is more complex than our claimed identities reveal to the rest of the world. One of the ways that the mind grapples with the complexity of the world and assesses whether difference is threatening is to operate in simple binaries, e.g., good or bad, black or white. Binaries make the world more manageable to our minds.

This is why the categories that we use to identify ourselves often start out in binary form: man or woman, gay or straight, majority or minority. These categories and labels are ones that we often cling to as a means of gaining a foothold in this world; we treat them as necessary to be seen, to claim a right to belong. In other words, our model of identity is built out of *opposition*.

Historically, this is true: Our models of racial identity and sexual orientation were constructed by the dominant group to draw boundaries and establish clear lines of difference from what then became the minority group. Identities by a dominant group are designed to avoid confusion with the "other." Those "others" in turn embrace and strengthen their identities in opposition to the majority. Faced with suppression and discrimination, minorities work to emancipate their identities by emphasizing that they are not lesser than the majority. This often takes the form of social and political organizing for increased legal protections, and through efforts to emphasize the dignity and value of the minority group (i.e., Gay Pride or Black Lives Matter).

There is nothing inherently wrong with this. As a gay man, I have greatly appreciated the efforts to extend legal protections to members of the LGBTQI community. But the Council's message is that it ultimately limits our capacity to move beyond our own constructed identities and out of a place of opposition. Our efforts to avoid difference and reduce the complexity of the world as we know it means that we rarely engage with the world as it really is. Our conversations are often responses to older patterns, former events, and childhood traumas that shape our perception of what's happening now and our expectations of how others should and will act. Various categories— race, gender, sexuality, nationality, etc.—that we have absorbed into our consciousness form part of our perceptions of other people. So we don't actually see the other person in their true nature, their "fullness"—the word the Council uses to describe the complexity and divinity of another person.

Rather, we see the world around us through the lens of the past, forged from old experiences, preconceived notions, and pre-set categories about how people should be and act. As a result, when we interact with other people, we are almost always talking to ghosts—to our memories of them from previous interactions, to similar people from other moments of our lives, and to the categories and labels we apply to those people. We are not engaging with them as they really are in the present moment. So powerful is our perception that it actually *creates* the present moment in the mold of the past. This is what the Council calls "bending time"—a term they also use in this book.

The key message of *Bending Time* was that humanity needs to stop turning the present moment into a version of the past. Instead, we must "bend" ourselves into the present moment by deepening our awareness of how much we see through the lens of the past and learning to let go of our frameworks and preconceived notions so that they don't shape our perceptions. We have to learn to open up to what appears before us with wonder and excitement, with fresh eyes, rather than imposing our memories, stories, assumptions, and expectations on the present moment. Bending time is not just about keeping our minds focused on the present. It is the practice of peeling back our habitual patterns and our mental concepts about what is appearing in front of us, in this very moment, to see the world as if we were seeing it for the first time.

Chief among our mental patterns is our perceived separation and fear of difference. Indeed, if we abandon our fear of difference and truly accept that we all belong here because we are all equally divine, then we do not need the identity categories that we so desperately cling to in order to demonstrate our worthiness and right to be here. Importantly, that approach also doesn't mean we need to be the *same*. It means our differences are not threatening, and that we can therefore celebrate them, and allow them to expand and flourish, as expressions of the infinite ways of being human—without claiming a sense of self in *opposition* to someone else's difference. That is the model of identity that we must release if we are to heal our world.

A world without identity is a world that is united by its shared commitment to that inexhaustible variety of human beings. When we embrace difference as the fundamental truth of who we are, then we will see our political, economic, legal, and social systems shift and transform, over time, into reflections of that diversity. Contrary to what the ego tells us, we will find unity by embracing difference. Our systems right now are a reflection of our fears around our differences. As we participate in those fields and ask how they can be more inclusive, and as we act with the belief that we are all one, those systems will come to reflect our inherent oneness. In the end, it is the intentionality with which we act—whether we speak and act from a place of unconditional love and oneness, or from a place of fear and division—that determines that evolution of our world. That is the power of our consciousness. At every moment, we are capable of recreating the world by taking actions that reflect our fundamental belief in our oneness. That is the fundamental teaching of this book.

TRANSMISSIONS

1

SOCIETY'S TRANSFORMATION

*T*his is the first installment of the final chapter in this three-part work. This will be a book unlike any other, as this one will directly address structures and aspects of your society that have never been the topic of channeled writing, for this is not usually how we wish to intervene in human affairs. But the time when we must engage you directly is now, so that you can prepare for a future that is unlike what you are now experiencing. This book will set forth new paradigms for a variety of structures in your society and culture, and for the planet as a whole. It will focus on several of the structures and institutions in your current world, and how those reflect the collective consciousness as it has come to be in the present moment. We will then explain how those institutions are in the process of evolving, and what will or must emerge.

We say "must" in the sense of what must occur if there is to be growth toward a new society. This new society is in the process of unfolding, and yet it requires your collective effort. It could not happen, because you are always free to exercise your will to choose a different path.

But the conditions have been set for a massive transformation, unlike anything that has ever occurred in the course of humanity's time on this planet. This moment is critical, as you face extinction in a short period of time if you do not change your current consciousness and transform your world. You are destroying the conditions that enable your survival on this planet, on Mother Gaia, and you are preparing to make it impossible for other Seeds of Light to incarnate here. We do not say this with any judgment or criticism, other than to point out that this is the logical consequence of your actions. As you move toward a certain death, you seem unable to grapple with the fact that you have chosen this path. Yes, you have chosen this path, by your allegiance to fear and separation, and your inability to embrace the truth of who you are.

This volume will demonstrate how you create societies that cannot survive, cannot function as humans were meant to function, and how you can function instead without separation and strife. You will need to develop something new, and that is what this book is going to lay out in detail. You will be the recipient of a new blueprint for how humanity is to evolve and how the structures that you currently use to organize and manage your collective lives are also going to need to undergo massive transformation. This can happen quickly, or it can happen slowly. That is always your free will and your willingness to move beyond the collective consciousness into which you are absorbed and that has captivated you for so long. The conditions are available for you to transcend it, and quickly, in the sense that you are all awakening, ever faster, and more and more of you are able to understand the truth of what it means to be a divine Seed of Light living in a human body.

Are you ready and willing to step up to confront the enormous challenge that faces you all, as a collective? It is our wish that you do so, and we are here to help you along this journey, to provide you with the tools necessary to see how you can create a new world, one born of compassion, rooted in the Christ Consciousness that sees no separation between one another, between all races and nations. All of those identities that you have used to gain a foothold in this realm, to give yourself a claim to authority or a claim to existence, are now going to fall by the wayside. For you do not need them, dear children, you do not need them to be seen.

We will show you what can and will rise from the remains of those structures of thought and identity that have captivated you for so long and yet never brought you the emancipation you so desperately seek. The answer is within your grasp, and we are here to assist you in this beautiful unfolding, this incredible ascension. You are living in an era that is seeing more transformation and experiencing higher frequencies of Light than any other. You are blessed, and we are a part of the blessing, and we will assist you in this transformation. Let us begin.

2

THE EGO AND THE TRUE SELF

*W*e *would like to start* with the basic structure of identity. This will be some overview and review for many of you, but it is important for understanding that the structures of your society are deeply reflective of the structures of identity that you have embraced and consolidated as part of mass consciousness.

The structure of identity that most of you come to know as the ego is based on the simple principle that the objects you see around you are separate from you in space and time. We have addressed in other works the elaborate relationship between space, time, and objects.[1] Suffice it to say that the way the mind works is to see other objects as separate from you, so that you are not one with the object. According to your mind, the rest of the world is always separate from you, both in space and time. This allows you to claim an existence, separate from all that you perceive.

The truth is that you are the consciousness that perceives all of it. That is the true you.

We have already reached the fundamental truth: You are all that you perceive, you are all that you experience, and you are all that is capable of being experienced as part of your perception, of your awareness of the universe. Yes, you are that vast. But the mind sees everything as solid and separate. You know that as matter of physics, nothing is truly solid; it is composed mostly of empty space, and there are lots of small units that make up matter. So while nothing is truly solid, the mind perceives the world as objects, varying in their solidity. You know that there is air, far less solid than stone or wood or steel. You know that materials can change form, such as water, which can be made frozen and solid, or made to boil and become steam. But despite knowing all of this and knowing that on some level, as a matter of physics, the world you experience is an illusion, a trick of the mind, played through the eyes, you continue to believe in it. You believe that you are solid and separate from all other objects, creatures, and creations, and so you act as if you're autonomous.

What this means is that all that exists in your awareness, which you view as separate from you, can easily continue without you. You can be extinguished from all of that, and the cars, and house, and plants, and clothes, and everybody else will just continue on afterward. Their existence does not depend on yours. Here, we are not talking about pain or the fact that you would be missed. We are not addressing the emotional impact that your death might cause. No, we are talking about whether their existence would continue if yours were to end. The mind says that you are not those objects, and you are not those people.

You can die, and they will continue. You can also continue, and they can die or disappear, and so you can experience loss as well. That is what the ego fundamentally depends on to claim its existence: a view of the world that says, *I exist because I am separate.* That separation depends on loss and death as its corollaries.

We begin with this overview because the foundational premise of this book is that the structures of your political realm, your legal system, and your economy all depend on this trope of separation. It is all designed based on this perception of the world and how to manage it. These are all structures born of the same consciousness that sees itself as existing in separation. These are, in short, all separation-based structures, and it is that fundamental foundation that makes them incapable of handling much of what is occurring on the planet now.

For what is upon you is a complete shift in how consciousness operates, as more and more of you divine Seeds of Light wake up and come to experience greater aspects of reality, and become aware of the vast possibilities for human consciousness. You begin to realize that the structures in place, which are designed to manage all of the problems that arise from separation, are fundamentally incapable of handling those problems any longer. They are no longer capable of handling the problem of separation because so many of you are waking up to the truth of who you are, and are no longer willing to accept a system based in separation. Where you once would have agreed with that system, you no longer do. You are moving toward unity, whether you realize it or not, as you seek to create a more inclusive society.

That is why you see breakdowns in your political and economic systems, and why your cultural realms seem so driven by strife and dissension and anger and hatred. Those of you who are invested in separation do not want to see these structures undone, for they provide you with what you believe you need. Yet these structures must give way for you to come into unity with one another. We are going to provide you, as we said, with an outline, a roadmap of how your changing consciousness must imagine and co-create new structures that reflect a deeper understanding of what it means to be human.

3

THE CORE EMOTION OF FEAR

*T*o understand why these structures no longer work, you must first understand how they are rooted in separation. The emotion at the core of separation is fear, and therefore fear is the thread that unites virtually every structure of thought and creation in your realm today. Yes, *fear*. The fear that comes from the belief in separation and that you can be harmed or killed, based on an identification of your mind with your body rather than an identification with awareness and the belief that you are an immortal Seed of Light. And so many of you deal with fear in so many ways, each and every day. We understand that you all experience loss, that you all experience the sense that you are no longer in control, that the possibility of loss is right around the corner. Fear is the frequency and register that runs throughout all of your social structures. You are all constantly straining to keep fear at bay, to keep it in check.

And so fear is the dominant note of every institution you build, from your schools to your houses, and your cities, and your stores, and virtually all of your spaces. You separate your physical world from one another, operating always and constantly with a certain level of fear. Your physical structures, used to house you, are designed to keep others out and to protect yourself from intruders. You use things called locks, to keep you safe. And all of your stores and institutions likewise shut doors and lock them, and put special bars on windows or chains on the doors, all to control the movement of people and things so that only certain people may be in certain places at certain times.

This is true of how you manage your schools, as well. You only allow certain people in at certain times and at certain ages, and then you arrange them in certain ways, so that they sit in certain positions and move from room to room at certain times, and cannot speak, and cannot do so much of what they would otherwise do freely. School is therefore where you begin to understand the inculcation of fear around your physical body and the vulnerability of your physical form, and the need for constant control and policing of the physical form.

For many of you reading this, you will say that they are the most vulnerable, they are children, and of course they must be protected. This is something that we understand—your impulse to love and protect—but realize that you are protecting them from your own creation, from the world that you have generated. Yes, they are vulnerable and in need of protection from *you*—from the mass consciousness that creates others as abusers, as those who would harm others, as those who would steal from others, and as those would deny each other their full access to life. And so you install all sorts of protective mechanisms to ensure your physical survival.

We see this as a manifestation of your deep absorption and rapture with separation. Look, for example, at all the ways you are physically controlled from space to space, in terms of where you can go and where you can't go and when you can go there, under what circumstances, and what you are allowed to do. You will begin to see how limited and confined you all are. Your movement in and through society is governed and limited so that you actually have very little to no access to most of your world.

Please begin to understand what it means that you have so little physical access, and how much of your world, in so many aspects, is completely dominated by fear. You are dominated by the fear of physical intrusion and harm, and by the fear of bodily integrity, of loss of physical life. You all regard each other as the possibility of being the one who damages or harms another, and must be protected against. Yes, you co-create each other as the enemy in the systems you inhabit.

Now, let us look more closely at schools, where you are taught so much about mass consciousness and are so inculcated into the ways of the collective. In schools, you are all lined up in nice rows with chairs and moved from box to box at prescribed times, with people telling you what you must do in each box. This seems efficient for ensuring that you maximize the time spent in learning, but you are also managing children in their infinite capacities, in their prolific and profound multiplicity, channeling and honing them into what is now the very limited model of what it means to be human in your realm. Yes, your schools, as institutions, are the primary locus for instilling the norms and mores of collective consciousness. The institution you call school, or education, is destined to facilitate your full immersion into the collective consciousness in a way that utterly narrows you to a mere trickle of Light from the shining beaming star light that you are when you arrive in form on this planet.

In your school system you teach students to adhere to certain norms and present themselves in certain ways, from where they sit and when they speak to how they dress. The school becomes the crucible for absorption into your society, and this is how you begin to prepare students, your children, to become the citizens you wish them to be. But this is a system that ultimately stultifies them. Yes, it provides them with information, but does it teach them about their minds, how to deal with their emotions, how to relate to other people other than through the conventions of the collective consciousness? No, it does not. That is how it has been designed.

A new design must come forward. Yes, a new design must come forward to allow children to begin to embody their Christ selves, their true selves, as Seeds of Light that can become something other than what the conventions say they must. For many children come out of school replicating what they have seen, for this is what your educating system does. It provides templates for replication. And children quickly decide that they want to be teachers or lawyers or astronauts. But how many of them say, *I want to be a psychic, I want to be an artist, I want to be a chef*, or *I want to do something that no one else has done*. Very few; so few that you extol those who demonstrate such amazing creativity, and yet you've done little to foster it. You are amazed at this wondrous creativity, when in fact almost every child could be that creative if your system allowed for it.

How can you begin to allow this to come forward? Allow them to be themselves. Allow them to be something other than what already exists. How often do you tell children that they can be anything that exists in the world and anything that doesn't yet exist in the world? How often is that the message? How often do you tell children that there are infinite possibilities, yet no one has exhausted them all, and that is why they are here? They are here to show us a new possibility, something hasn't been done before. This is never the message. And so you do not enable their creative faculties to shine.

No, you try to constrain and contain their energies. When they prove unruly, when they do not fit the cloistered box you call "education," they must be given drugs, sedatives, something to contain and focus them. Why the need for focus? Allow them to explore, set up the possibility that what is needed is something else, provide the parameters necessary to ensure the child's physical wellbeing, and then let them go.

We are not saying there can be no formal teaching, no learning of rote information. This is necessary to be able to engage and converse and operate with the rest of the world, but it does not need to be coupled with a view of the world that seeks to constrain and contain the source energy that children embody. That is where you must begin to allow for greater possibility where currently there is none.

4

THE NEED FOR APPROVAL

*A*s we have said, *through* your schools you educate people on the need to control the flow of bodies in and through your world, teaching you that you can only go to certain places at certain times, and that you must remain where you are told you can go. This control of the body, of the physical form, dominates virtually every aspect of your life, dictating where you can and cannot go. We understand that for most of you, this is a necessary means of ensuring that you respect the separation and free will of another body, and do not infringe on its ability to remain separate from all else. For that is the definition of free will: the ability to maintain your separation, your physical separation, from all other beings in this realm.

And so you have all sorts of means of directing the flow of people, from cars and streets to homes and sidewalks, dictating where they can and cannot go. So much of your physical realm is designed to manage how people move in space and time in relationship to each other, ensuring that the body can move. We do not question or challenge this. Rather, we are here to point out the many ways that your bodies are required, from the outset of your life, to adhere to a very limited set of norms, and how the body is consistently made to adhere to that certain set of parameters. You cannot go in this direction, you cannot go here, and you must behave in this way. You do this with your mannerisms and the ways in which your body is allowed to express the energy of life. You tamper its enthusiasm, its energy, so that it flows in a mere trickle, and is contained, highly reserved. You are allowed to express your body's deep joy only in very limited circumstances, and in ways that are "socially acceptable," and you begin to teach this at an early age in school.

That is why we began with your institutions of learning, for your institutions are equally part of mass consciousness, and the collective consciousness teaches you to contain yourself, to adhere to certain norms, that, while designed to ensure survival, end up limiting life in many deep and profound ways. As we explained in our previous transmission, your schools teach children very limited ways of engaging with each other, and they are rewarded for positive behavior and punished for negative behavior. No doubt many of you will say that this social learning is required, and it is necessary for a functioning society. We say that the learning process is inevitable, but the type of society in which you absorb all younglings in your world is not a requirement.

No, you have constructed a world based on your view of what it means to be human, and so your institutions reflect that view. The institution of the elementary school, which teaches children the elementary building blocks of human interaction and relationship, is built on the edifice of your views on separation. And so you teach children "good manners." Yes, that is true. But you also teach them other habits, about what they can and cannot do with their bodies, how they must express themselves in very limited ways, and how they cannot express themselves in other ways without the threat to their physical wellbeing, through some sort of physical punishment or isolation or simply what is acceptable and permitted. Yes, that is what you do very quickly with your children: You insert them into the collective consciousness and inculcate them with all manner of values of what it means to be in a human body.

This approach to human education instills in them a deep fear of disapproval early on. That is the place where the approval mechanism begins, although it obviously also begins in the home, where the parents themselves have this same deep sense of needing approval, having learned it from their parents and school as well. Approval means that you do not make a mistake and somehow incur the wrath of the teacher, the figure who stands in authority over the students. You wonder why you always want to curry favor and seek approval. It begins here, at the earliest age, with the figure of authority who sets rules and organizes bodies, and who then arranges you according to a hierarchy of how well you have done on your homework or your tests or how well you have played with others, and how well you have adhered to the range of expressions that you are permitted to have. Approval means you conform to the model of human subjectivity presented by this figure of authority, who does not necessarily mean to instill these aspects and may believe that they are actually encouraging your full blossoming. But how can they really encourage that when they too are a product of the collective consciousness, and do not see their divinity or their children's divinity in its fullness? No, they are repeating and creating that which came before them.

But it is important to understand that the earliest moments of your life set up this paradigm of a figure of authority—a central figure of authority who establishes rules and organizes bodies and dictates where and when they can move and how they might express themselves, and what will occur if they do not adhere to these norms. This instills a very profound fear of punishment and a deep need for approval, to satisfy the teacher so that no harm will come to the physical body. This is the crux of your earliest education, the core principle, upon which is layered many more ideas about what it means to be human.

We begin here because you will see that this core principle extends to virtually every arena in the rest of your realm, in the rest of your physical world, that you occupy. And it is this core principle that must be dismantled and reworked so that a new relationship, a new paradigm—one where divinity, the fullness of what it means to be human, can flourish and emerge, in a way that is not driven by the collective consciousness, so that fear and approval are not the twin guides for your interactions. We will say more on how the paradigm must shift, but for now we close with the understanding that this core concern is this central figure of authority from whom all rules and laws emanate, and who will dictate and control your relationship to all other beings.

5

WHEN LIFE BEGINS

*A*s *we've already said, the* basic institution of education establishes certain parameters and dictates for approval and punishment, and for how your body must exist in relationship to all other bodies. That same principle around punishment and approval is at the core of another aspect of human life that many you struggle with, as well. This is the topic of abortion, and what it means to make the decision to terminate a pregnancy.

Gestation is the process by which human cells coalesce to form a separate human entity, and this human entity starts out as a fusion of cells within the mother's body, with the DNA supplied by the father, and this unfolds in ways that you all well know, because this is the basic structure for humanity's growth and survival. In short, you have babies.

This gestation process is one in which the baby is housed within the mother until the child is ready to come into this world and exist as a separate entity, and experience time and space like everyone else. For until then, while the child is growing, it does not experience time and space in the same way. It may experience stimuli from the external world, and in relation to the mother's own body, but the child has no concept of time at that point. It is merely experiencing whatever it experiences in the here and the now, and as it does from each second to the next, and this experience does not cause it to reflect or fear or anticipate or engage in any mental activity.

Gestation then is the liminal state between non-form and separation; it is the place where you exist in form but are not yet separate and have no concept of time and space. It is this in-between phase when you have moved out to the realm of the spirit or Light and into a physical body, and yet you are not separate, you do not yet exist apart from the mother in any conceptual way. That comes later, once you have entered the world and perceive yourself as separate from others in both time and space.

This period of life for so many of you creates any number of confusions about what the child means and whether it's alive— yes, it is alive from the moment the mother becomes pregnant— and you expend copious amounts of energy on whether it is okay to end that life, or whether you must carry the child to term, or whether you condemn the child to some sort of eternal damnation or condemn the mother to eternal damnation if you allow this to happen. You ask questions like *When does the child have a soul?*, or *What is the moment when the child is viable and therefore separate from the body?*

We can tell you now that the notion of viability as a means of marking when the child is separate from the mother seems logical, but has no real anchor in reality. No, for you have privileged separation as the touchstone for when the child has a life of its own worth protecting, and this is not the moment. There is life in the child from the outset. The cells that are moving and forming are indeed the place where the child is already alive, in the sense that the energy of life is coming together and coalescing to create a new entity. This is the primary function of the gestation process, as you well know: to allow the child to form a single, physical body in which it can then exist separately.

We understand why your society privileges viability as the marker for when the child is alive and somehow separate, but we are here to tell you that this is not the moment when life starts to exist and the previous line, a time when the child is not yet ready to exist separate from the mother, is somehow "not life." This is a mistake in understanding the nature of human existence, and we will not tell you that you are not killing when you have an abortion prior to the moment of viability as you have defined it.

Patrick is deeply uncomfortable with all of this because he comes from a liberal background that says it is the woman's choice to have an abortion, and that has rejected for some time the conservative view of many members of your society, who speak in the name of God and say that abortion is not permitted and is a sin, and that the mother should have no choice.

And we are here to tell you that neither position is accurate.

Yes, it is the woman's choice, always; this is free will. You have free will in this realm, but do not believe that you are not destroying life. You destroy life when you kill a bug, and it would be no different to kill a creation that has yet to separate from you but is quite obviously full of the energy of life. But this is not an issue of eternal damnation or the soul of the child being cast into some nether realm. That is not accurate either. You are simply falling prey to a fear-based model of what it means to be human and how humans relate to the Light.

Can you not see that there is a very simple away to understand this? The child is alive, and you have the choice to terminate that life, as with all life, and you will face the karmic consequences. Patrick says that this sounds like judgment, like you will be punished. And we are not saying this, for there is no punishment. No, we are saying that there is a karmic consequence to the mother, for her own emotional wellbeing, that this child's life stream is ended prematurely, or before it is allowed to separate from the mother.

Are we suggesting that you cannot engage in this practice called abortion? No, we are not, because we are not here to deprive you of free will. But we are here to tell you that there is life in that creation, that the moment of gestation marks the moment of a creation of life, and that you cannot rationalize your decision based on some artificial notion of viability as the marker of when it is okay or not. You must contend with the fact that you have utilized your will to cut short a life stream in formation, and that this life stream is a Seed of Light, is a sliver of the Creator, and that its soul will then no longer occupy that form. It may barely occupy that form, for even the smallest amount of time, before the abortion ends the physical gestational process and the soul leaves those cells.

But understand that the soul that wished to incarnate also had a soul purpose, and had a reason for coming into this realm, and while you can choose not to follow through with that process, understand that you do not know the purpose for which that soul may have sought to incarnate in that way, in that manner, in that mother, and therefore you cannot fully appreciate the role that the child would have played in the mother's life or in this world.

We do not say this to create guilt in any mothers who have opted to terminate their pregnancies, and we acknowledge that Patrick is uncomfortable with this topic, but that is the truth as the Council of Light can proclaim it: There is life in that fetus, and the soul's purpose must then find a new vehicle, a new path, to form in this realm.

Patrick is wondering why we have spoken of abortion, and we have said that this book will be about many of the most controversial topics that afflict your society, and the institutions you have built up around them, and this topic, perhaps more so than any other, divides and occupies you. We wish to begin with a topic that makes Patrick uncomfortable because it is through that discomfort that you must all pass. You must all learn to acknowledge your discomfort with the actions that you take as humans in form, and to acknowledge that you are not always in alignment with all of life.

That is okay. That is what you are learning. You are then able to recognize the ways that you engage in rationalizations of your behavior—ways that are rooted in separation and that govern how you regulate the behavior of others. This is clear here with abortion, where the line you have drawn in your society, in the United States, is so-called *viability*: a line that marks when the child could survive if separated from the mother. You see how clearly you have chosen the very notion of separation and survival as the mark of when it would be okay to terminate a pregnancy and when not to. By doing so, you can see how you privilege separation as a principle for organizing your world.

With that we will conclude for today so that you can begin to see where else in your life you privilege separation in your institutions and make survival and separation the touchstones for how you rationalize your behavior. For those concerns infiltrate virtually every dimension of your realm, as you have constructed it.

6

RESPONSIBILITY FOR THE WHOLE

*A*s *much as you are* occupied with your own survival and rely on the concept of separation to justify where you believe life begins, the thread that actually binds all of you is the responsibility you have to each other. You do not fully appreciate your responsibility to each other. You use your categories of identity to determine where you are responsible and to rank on a hierarchy your responsibility to others. So you are more responsible to your family, and less responsible to strangers, and more responsible to your neighbors and less responsible to people who live far away. And we understand that your capacity to embrace everyone as your responsibility seems daunting and overwhelming, if not impossible.

How can we be responsible for everyone? If we do that, we will not take care of ourselves, and we won't be able to be responsible for anyone.[1]

This is what you say, and this is matter of degree. It is a matter of how you perceive your actions. You envision that your responsibility to each other requires that you undertake the same actions for everyone that you take for your family or coworkers, but this is not true. This is not about you undertaking the same actions, like you having to clean up the dishes or take out the garbage for your neighbors or fellow citizens of whatever political structure you envision for yourself.

That is not what we mean. That is where you commit an error and misperceive what it means to be responsible for everyone. It involves a change of mindset, which means that you regard yourself in relation to all others, and look at your actions in relationship to all others. You assume that your actions have impacts on others, including others that you do not see, and that your sense of responsibility is to ensure that your actions are designed to not burden others. And this means that you do things that seem inconvenient, or you do things with the knowledge that they may benefit others. The principle here is to undertake your actions with a greater awareness of the whole in which you operate. That should alter not only what you do but also how you do it. Yes, that is your responsibility to others.

You cannot assume that your actions have no impact, and you cannot assume that if you don't want to do something, it will be done by someone else. That is what we mean when we say you must have responsibility for everyone, rather than just yourself and those close to you.

This also changes how you relate to the structures that make up your society. It alters whether you regard events that occur or structures that are in place as having any relevance to your life. Everything is relevant to your life when you are aware of it, because it means that it is part of you. *For you are your aware-ness.* You are not your thoughts or judgments about it, you are not the body that you are housed in. That is, as we have said, the vehicle through which you experience this physical realm. And you are not your personality or identity. These are parts of the collective consciousness, and how you relate to them is a measure of your absorption into that consciousness. No, you are *awareness*. That is the true you: the awareness of all that is within your perception.

Can you imagine how vast you are? Whenever you think about some aspect of your world, when you are aware of it, you are experiencing your perception—*and everything you perceive is a part of you.* It is your awareness, the vast consciousness that you are, that is your Light, that encompasses and embraces all that can come within it. So when you undertake to see all that you are aware of as your responsibility, you are beginning to re-late to the world around you differently. You no longer regard it as "not you" because it does not affect you directly, or isn't about your identity. No, that is the way of the collective, mass consciousness, that separates and divides, and says, *That's not me, and that's not my responsibility.*

It is *all* your responsibility, and this shift means that when something occurs in the world, you must ask yourself, *Where am I resonating with this? Where do I engage in the same actions, in some parallel way, even if just a to degree?* For it is that reso-nance that allows you to contain it as part of your awareness.

How do you begin to relate to the whole as your responsi-bility? As we said, you begin to ask where you are in relation to it, where you resonate with it even in the smallest way. And you begin to regard your actions as always in relationship to another, and to all others. How does your choice involve another person? When you stop to think about it, everything you do involves an impact on another person—at least one other person in your realm, and often many, many people. In this way, you can begin to recognize that you are not separate from each other.

See how your actions, from the simplest task of eating or drinking water, to taking out the garbage or riding a subway, to driving on a highway, involve other people, involve you coordinating with them and obeying the same rules so that you can all be in harmony with each other. Who picks up your garbage? Who prepares your food? Who takes care of the water systems that you enjoy each day? Who takes care of the roads? Who, who, who? When you begin to see yourself as part of this intricate and beautiful web of lights all dancing together, then you can begin to see that you are responsible for all of them, and they for you, for this goes hand in hand.

This is what is meant by co-creating each other. You must co-create each other now with that sense of mutual responsibility, with a sense that what you do affects the other, and vice versa. That is the start, the starting point, for a new society of constant awareness of mutual responsibility, an awareness of each other. For you are, in that awareness, each other.

7

POLITICAL IDENTIFICATIONS

*T*hat *sense of awareness and* responsibility to everyone does not yet shape your political system. On the contrary, the political system that you have created is built upon the edifice of separation that we call the collective consciousness. We will speak of the binaries that make up your party system, and how you are unable to speak of more than two parties in the United States, as this creates all sorts of linguistic and intellectual confusion about who you are and how to envision yourself as a nation, and that this is part of the dilemma.

But we wish to speak first of a more elementary issue that beleaguers your political system: *identification.* So much of your system of politics is built upon identification. With whom do you identify? And by *identification*, you tend to mean with whom are you alike, who resembles you in some way, and can you therefore connect with this person.

Do you not see that this is the framework for how you regard the entire world? You regard each other as either other or as the same, as like you or not like you. It therefore follows that your political system would suffer from the same issue: You do the same with the people who you have chosen to represent you as part of a political system based on some people speaking for the voices of many other people. That is your system, this representative system, that requires some to speak for others, and yet you ask that this person resemble you, *Be like me in some way, and I will allow you to speak for me.*

For this is based on the notion that you cannot possibly connect with or be in alignment with someone who does not resemble you, or somehow violates your sense of what the "right" way to be is. And we do not say that this is wrong, we do not say that it does not comport with elementary logic to ask that the person who speaks on your behalf to actually share the same views, but that is not what you do. No, you ask that this person *resemble* you in many ways that have nothing to do with the logic of political representation, with the very issues that you would ask them to speak to. You ask them to resemble you in ways that have nothing to do with that, but whether you can somehow relate to this person and see yourself in them.

That is how you relate to each other, and so you expect them to behave in ways that have little do with the job to be performed. You want them to make you feel comfortable, to feel at home, to be your friend, the person you can invite to a BBQ or whatever social event would make you feel connected to this person. You wish this person to be a friend in some way, a surrogate for some other relationship in your life, something else that makes you feel alive, rather than someone who will speak to certain political issues.

The answer to this is to simply relinquish your belief that the other person is someone that you would need to know and relate to as you would a friend. This is the first step in beginning to see the ways in which you evaluate the people who speak on your behalf. Do you ask them to connect with you in the ways that matter for the office? Or do you ask them to connect with you in ways that would allow you to enjoy their social company?

Don't people use that as a means of testing trustworthiness?

Yes, and we will speak to trust, which is something that bedevils all of your relationships. It is primarily that way of thinking that leads you to try to relate to them as friends, to allow the imagined bond of friendship between you and the politician to serve as the proxy for trust—not whether they in fact will speak to the issues, but whether they will violate the bond of trust that friendship entails. But there is no friendship. This is all imagined in your head, a fantasy relationship based on how this person behaves so that you draw the conclusion, *Oh, I could connect with this person, and so I can trust her, too.*

You seek to relate to politicians by how they make you feel. That they treat you and speak to you in ways that suggest you can identify with them, that you share certain commonalities with them, is the means by which you evaluate them and predict their future behavior, and therefore think you can trust them. And this is the fundamental problem. You cannot in any way anticipate what they will do based on how they make you feel about yourself. If you feel that this person is someone who you could connect with in a social setting, or who you think conforms to certain ideals because of their qualities that have nothing to do with the position for which they are seeking, then you are making a critical error in judgment.

You do not need to identify with them in the way that you do, and in fact, this creates all sorts of difficulties, for then you wonder why a person behaves a particular way when in fact, you've decided that they would and should behave in a particular way based on your mental projection of what this person, your political representative, must be like.

And this is fundamentally done to ensure what you believe is called trustworthiness. In reality, it is not trust that you seek, but rather prediction and security. You believe that the outcome can be determined in advance according to the views that they supposedly share with you. And this is what your political system is designed to do: make you feel certain that you can place your trust in this person and give them your vote because they are like you in some way.

And this is folly, we say, for the very notion that you have someone speaking on your behalf means that regardless of how you feel about them, they should speak on your behalf. They should represent your views, and to choose politicians based on how they make you feel rather than how they will vote according to their values and viewpoints means that you cannot possibly feel critical about their choices. No, you have opted for identification over representation as a way of relating to politicians.

※

The choice you make with a politician is often fundamentally at odds with the values that you actually espouse. That is a difficult conundrum, and it is due in part to the structure, the binary structure, that governs most of your political system. First and foremost, the political parties, which are deeply entrenched in their respective positions, even as new contenders come along, or the parties shift, remain the political entities with the most power to shape the electoral landscape. And so understand that from the outset, the very notion that you have two choices and only two choices inevitably creates situations where your views are never going to be reflected. No, your views will be subordinated to the party machinery that exists to ensure that the party continues.

Understand that this is the way all binaries work. For once your system came to be dominated by a binary structure of two parties, your vote for someone is always really a choice made not only in support of a candidate but also in opposition to someone else. This is always the case, except where there are third parties, but your collective consciousness lacks the imagination and suppleness to be able to adequately think through how three parties of equal strength would operate.

❄

You may question whether we have fully explained why identification is an issue and how this relates to the political system as it currently exists in the United States. You may question whether you can escape identification altogether, and whether there are other means to determine whether someone is going to adhere to the values that you espouse. You have no solution to this as your system exists, because your system does not actually allow for a person to represent your views.

You identify with people based on how they make you feel and whether you believe they will be trustworthy or adhere to your views. And you do this because your representatives are not actually beholden to you. This is the fiction that you all have created to determine whether or not you are in alignment with your belief in democracy. That is, you have constructed a system in which people appear to choose others to represent their views, when in fact you know that you do not. You do not have a system of representative democracy. No, you have a system of corporate democracy, where the politicians that you have "chosen" are actually in the hands of a legal fiction that you have also created, something called a corporation. So you have one legal fiction built upon another legal fiction.

That means that you choose people based on what you think they are like as individuals, without fully acknowledging the multiple ways that these people are merely functionaries for yet another legal entity.

This sounds cynical.

We are not cynical. We are descriptive. The politicians who govern you as a country are actually responding to the interests of those who wield the power to ensure that those politicians remain in their position. And those are, by and large, the legal fiction you call corporations, whose purpose is precisely to grow capital, to grow money. So it makes perfect sense. You have allowed yourselves to generate a system that says that money is speech, and that speech cannot be controlled or regulated, and that means the legal entities that are designed to be most effective at creating money are now also the most effective at creating and generating speech.

Those who are chosen to listen to those who speak are listening to those who speak the most, and most clearly—that is, the corporations. How could it be otherwise? You have constructed this perfectly, brilliantly. It is the perfect manifestation of your belief systems. The ways that you have constructed your society are consistent with your beliefs about what it means to be a member of your society. That is, being a member of your society comes with all sorts of beliefs of what it means to be "American," and this is what allows you to generate the type of political structure you have.

We will elaborate. You have a series of values that you have generated, and a series of a concepts that comprise the identity of "American," and out of that you have constructed a series of groups, which you call parties, around which you can organize. These parties each then vie for the title of which represents most accurately and fully the identity that you have all agreed upon is "American," and so one group claims to be more representative of "America" than the other and you debate endlessly what it means to be "American" and whether one group or another is the most representative.

Then you "choose" based on this notion, when in fact it is the corporations who most speak to them, and they speak a language that is rooted in certain aspects of your American identity, particularly the aspects around capitalism, individual authority, enterprise, etc. You believe strongly in innovation and growth and expansion. These are part of your American identity, and they infuse the concept of the corporation as well.

Understand, then, that your system is based on your personal identification with the individual politicians and on identification with a concept of "America." Those concepts that have made up this identity known as America have led you to construct a political system that is perfectly consistent with those principles. And the end result is that you have generated a series of legal fictions out of the fabric of that identity that have served to tell you that you have representative democracy, when in fact you have a capitalist-driven corporate democracy that is controlled by the entities that have accumulated the most speech. You use—or misuse, to be more precise—identification in the political realm to manage your fundamental belief in separation, which in turn blinds you to the reality that the legal fictions you have created are actually in charge of your political system.

8

CORPORATE FICTIONS

*A*s *we've just seen, you* have created a system that privileges certain types of speech, and in so doing, have created a system in which the very entities that are responsible for so many of the problems in your society are themselves able to influence that society so greatly, so profoundly. We are speaking, again, of your legal fiction known as the corporate structure.

The corporate structure is simply a mechanism, crafted in language, that says that this entity, this thing that exists in language but does not have a single physical form anywhere in the universe, has an existence. And that existence has a claim to all of the protections and rights that are normally afforded an entity that occupies a single physical form. The corporate form is permitted to speak, enter contracts, negotiate in language, and do all sorts of things. It is a product of language, it exists as language, as an agreement. You have *agreed* that these structures, these entities, exist so that people can give over their resources and claim to own a piece of the entity, and in return, they are permitted to receive a portion of what the entity earns. It is a means of pooling resources and allowing that entity to accumulate resources by engaging in commerce.

But the fact remains that this entity is nothing but a creation of language, and does not have an existence separate and apart from the agreement that you have created.

You imbue that entity with all manner of agency and consciousness. You act as if the corporate entity, which exists solely to accumulate funds, has the right to "speak," as if it had a consciousness separate and apart from the consciousness of those who are running the entity. You act as if not letting the corporation exercise that right would somehow undermine its existence. Lacking a physical form, the corporate entity is nothing but a subterfuge for those who would use it to pool resources and then use those resources to allow the corporate form to accumulate even more.

You act as if this were a great mystery, and you act as if corporations had a consciousness of their own, and they do, insofar as they take on and become their own being by virtue of the agreement that they exist as such. But only as that agreement. They are not human; they are not Seeds of Light, they have no soul, and they are not here to learn to love. They are incapable of love. They are a legal fiction, a fabrication made of words, and yet you imbue them with more existence than the many people who do exist in physical form in this realm.

Why do you do that? Because so many people come to identify with the corporate form, and earn their living through the corporate form, they cannot imagine standing up to the corporate form for it would hinder their own earning potential. It would eliminate their foundation for survival and existence in this realm. In short, their own belief in separation anchors their attachment to the corporate form as their means to earn money and make a living.

Beholden to the corporate form, you continue the illusion that corporations are entitled to the same rights and protections as a living human being. The result is madness, of course, and you witness that madness on a daily basis when you learn that corporations have been responsible for horrific ecological disasters or are oblivious to climate change, do little to respect the law and often attempt to wield massive influence over the political system, all in an effort to protect their own interests, and thereby the interests of the human beings who happen to be running them, who use the corporate form to their own advantage.

That is what occurs: The corporate form is an example of individual human beings using their creative potential in the service of their own survival, of using language—the medium you all use to navigate separation—as a means of co-creating something that allows them to accumulate a great deal of resources and to wield those resources without fear of oversight or restriction. This is an example of your creative powers, so creative, being pressed into the service of the ego and the need to survive based on a fear rooted in separation.

The corporate form does not need to exist. It is your invention, your creation, and you can easily imagine or create something new, some other structure for organizing yourselves to undertake commerce that does not result in the corporate form itself becoming the dominant force in your political system.

Part of your transformation will involve imagining and calling into being other ways of organizing yourselves not founded on the principle of separation or by treating your legal creations as having the status of a person.

9

MASS INCARCERATION

J ust as the corporation is not necessary, neither is your approach to incarceration and punishment, in which you
literally separate people from the rest of the world. As we
have said, your society is erected on a foundation of separation;
the structures that you use to govern your relationships are all
built on separation. The same is true for how you punish people.
For those who are instilled in the world of separation often act
out in ways that do not reflect their divine status, and so they
cheat or hurt or murder others, and they do so because they do
not know who they are, and they treat each other as objects, like
anything else that is separate from them in the world. In turn,
you treat them as objects by isolating them and by separating
them. Your response to an act of aggression, rooted in separation, is further isolating the perpetrator, through imprisonment.

Do you not see the folly in this? Do you not see that you
merely compound this issue by furthering their sense of

isolation? For that is what led them to undertake those actions to begin with. They did not feel connected to the rest of the world, they were immersed in separation, in the belief that they were isolated and separate from all, and therefore to survive they had to undertake certain actions. Their absorption in the collective consciousness infused them with a host of beliefs about what the world is like and how people should be, and this fueled their actions as well.

When your response to this situation is to further isolate them, it means that they never experience the kind of integration they need to release their anger and fear at the world that seems to treat them so badly. Do you not see this in the massive rates of recidivism among those you have isolated through prison time? Do you not see that they never feel reintegrated into a community? No, they do not. They struggle with their separation and fall back into the same patterns as before. This is the insane response you have to a situation that stems from the basic principle of all human consciousness. How ironic that you should choose to respond in the same way, with the very same structure of thought that governs all of you.

Can you see the irony in that the very reasons for their misguided behavior, for their lack of respect for someone else, is their separation? Do you believe they would have committed their wrong if they did not feel and act as if they were separate from the rest of the world? No, and so your response to criminality is to separate. That is, you regard the individual as having committed some wrong and that the solution is to ensure that they cannot repeat it by enclosing them in time and space, to cleave them from the rest of society so that they may not interact with the rest of the physical realm in the same way.

By doing this, you make them feel like they do not belong. You brand them as criminals. You impose on them all sorts of conditions and constraints that remind them that they are not a part of society, that they are separate, and then you wonder why they do what they do, or why they do not integrate. For when they do not behave according to your dictates and norms, you separate them again, and make them solitary, and there are all sorts of pernicious emotional effects from such isolation. Yes, isolation does nothing but harm them more and deepen their sense of separation and isolation, which is the core of the reason why they misbehaved in the first place. So we regard your system of handling wrongdoing as utter folly, complete and utter folly.

If you could only see that the way they respond to the demands placed upon by them by the collective consciousness, which tells them that they are not good enough, do not belong, and are not worthy of love and abundance, is to resort to misguided actions that you have labeled crimes, then you would see that what they need in response is not to be isolated and told again that they are wrong, but full and complete integration into a community that affords them the love they were denied at the outset.

What would that look like? You already have models of rehabilitation that are centered on forgiveness and community reintegration.[1] But you are driven by fear, fear that this won't work, fear that if you allow them to wander the streets, they will misbehave again. Yet this is the case already. The rates of recidivism are enormous. Anyone who is branded a criminal has a fairly high chance of committing another crime, because you as a collective have operated from fear and separation and do nothing to integrate them. They are left believing they have no options. They cannot find work, and they often lack the skills to do something other than commit the very same crime that landed them in prison in the first place.

So what you must do is recognize that your current system of incarceration is grounded in your own self-preservation, in your own desire to be safe from what you perceive to be a threat, rather than taking collective responsibility for this person's behavior. Yes, take responsibility. It is your responsibility. You have all co-created each other, and so it is your responsibility to ensure that this person is forgiven and feels love. This is the way to avoid more misguided behavior. You already have models of this in other societies, where the response to wrongdoing is not expulsion and incarceration, but forgiveness and reconciliation. That is the path to ensuring a society that does not continue to operate on separation.

Do you not see as well that you do the same with the ways in which you refuse to contemplate and grapple with the past? Do you not see that your mode of responding to issues such as the collective harm to blacks in your society should be accounted for, and yet you do nothing to actually heal that wound? No, there is no reintegration into society as a whole, never any acknowledgement of the harm done. Instead, you act as if the fault belonged to someone else; it was the result of another, and not your responsibility. And we have spoken about how the entire world, all of it, is your responsibility, and that it is the refusal to act on this responsibility that contributes to the prevalence of the same mechanisms, the same structures, that continue to replicate the sense of separation. And so you have a society in which those who descended from slaves now grapple with prison time from policies based on separation. Do you not see the madness in this? You still have policies that unfairly target blacks in your society, that send them to jail in highly disproportionate numbers, that never acknowledge the legacy of slavery in this country.

Do you not see that a massive form of forgiveness and reconciliation is what is required of you? It is the affirmative recognition of and forgiveness that must take place on a global scale really, for this not to replicate itself. For you continue to replicate yourselves according to this legacy of slavery, this consciousness that is rooted in the belief in the separation of people along racial lines, and we tell you now, and we have said it before, this is utter madness. It is folly. This separation is a convention that will never lead to your happiness, for anyone. It is a convention you have all created based on pigmentation in your skins, and you do not need this identity to protect those who have been harmed, and you do not need to divide each other up in this way to exist, but that is what you do.

And so you must begin to reconcile by acknowledging that these racial divisions have been built to subordinate, to harm others whom you, on a collective level, have decided are less worthy of the full range of experience, who have less of a claim to existence in this realm. You must honor and acknowledge this as a collective for there to ever be full peace, and for race to be dismantled as a product of the ego that privileges what your eyes tell you in ways that do not reflect your fullness as humans, as Seeds of Light.

This is what we are telling you: Your modes of handling conflict that result from separation are often still rooted in separation. This is especially true for how you incarcerate certain races more than others. You must embrace a new way of handling these conflicts, by embracing modes of forgiveness on larger scales, by honoring and acknowledging the past harm that you've done, so that you can begin to move forward and shed these artificially constraining categories that serve only to limit you, to limit the range of human experience available to you. That is the only way, and we will expand on why the law does what it can but is incomplete, and we will elaborate on how these aspects of separation permeate your political, economic, and legal structures. For now, understand that your perception of your fellow humans must always recognize the wholeness, the fullness of another, and never solely the partial and limited categories to which you've assigned them as part of your belief in separation.

10

ECONOMIC INEQUALITY

*W*e *have already alluded in* our discussion of politicians to how capitalism, as your economic structure, is the foundation upon which your economy works, and thus how you work with the energy known as money. Here we wish to underscore how you conceptualize and use money to manage your separation from one another. You can use many types of currency or objects of value for exchange. You could trade and barter, you could use gold, but you have instead created a symbolic system known as money or currency, that supposedly reflects a certain amount of a precious material but is in fact now just a symbolic valuation of what you think something should earn.

This is the structure to which you have agreed, and you are focused almost entirely on the accumulation of that type of currency or money. Much of your current struggles have to do with money. Your politicians spend much time discussing income inequality and the ways they are going to shift the structure so that many more people have access to money. And we are here to tell you that this will never change as a result of your proposed changes to your system, which is designed to allow a very small percentage of people to accumulate and control vast amounts of that energy. That is all money really is: the co-creation of a certain type of energy in your realm. Like language, it is a form of energy transfer between you, but whereas language is used to communicate, money is used to transfer other energy, in the form of goods and services. And in that regard, you might think of money as simply the mechanism for creation— the source or energy that allows you to spend it and in exchange obtain a physical object or some other aspect of your realm that you would not have been able to acquire otherwise.

Money, as we have explained elsewhere, is not at all the source of wrong.[1] The source of wrong is rather the minds that use and control the flow of money, and so it is your *relationship* to money that you struggle with. Your current system allows for objects and services to be valued, to be given a price tag, and then people can decide whether to buy them.

Your system also allows people to set the valuation of a certain type of instrument, of certain objects that themselves have no independent value. This is how your Wall Street works, setting up these objects that have no independent value except that someone else says this is what they are worth, and then someone else buys or sells depending on whether they think that this will make or lose money. Your system is little more than a structure around betting. Something similar occurs with the realm of the commodity, of the precious object that you idealize, like fashion or art or cars, or anything really, where there are a select few who have somehow been chosen to assign value, and they tell you that this object is worth a great deal more than this other object. You wear that dress, and it is worth much more energy than this other dress that requires only a little bit of energy to obtain. Your structure is built on this valuation of objects that ranks them according to whether they are worth or more or less than something else.

Do you see that your entire system is based on the same structure of the mind that sees value and difference in everything else, but most importantly, in other people? Do you not see that you are essentially engaging in a certain judgment of all the physical world and assigning it value, and then deciding that the value that is assigned to a certain set of objects is worth a certain amount of this particular energy you call money, and that if you supply that energy, you can acquire this thing? That is your system, and it is based on the notion that you are free to offer these things, and people will choose, and you will then be able to acquire, as the seller, vast amounts of this energy called money.

All of this is built on principles of differentiation and valuation, of offering something that is different and better than something else. This object people want; this other object people don't want. This system perpetuates your belief in separation by placing everything in a hierarchy of value—a hierarchy that is often set by the very people who have the most money or set in ways that have little to do with the true value of those objects.

�֎

In addition to assigning different monetary values to different objects, you have erected certain structures that are designed to facilitate the flow and exchange of that money. But just as valuation is not equal, money itself does not flow freely, and it does not flow equally. No, it flows according to parameters set by those in power who wish to accumulate money.

The same core belief around separation drives your relationship to money. Much of your political system is occupied with the transfer of wealth. The transfer of wealth occurs when the political system accumulates wealth and then distributes it. It takes in money through taxes and then sends that money to various departments and locales, including cities and states. How do you decide that some monies should go here and others should go there? Well, this is all done based on the bargaining that occurs in your political system, and this bargaining occurs among the very same actors who are themselves beholden to certain interests that have influenced them because of their ability to accumulate vast amounts of money. So again, we are simply identifying and noting that those who can accumulate money can dictate to those who are in a position to determine where money from taxation next flows. So money accumulates power, and those with power and money can then influence the distribution of that money.

Let us turn briefly to taxation, and how money comes into the federal government in the United States. The money is accumulated through a mechanism that requires everybody to ascertain how much money they have, and then they are supposed to determine how much of that to share with the federal government, who in turn would redistribute it according to certain needs. So you can see that there is right away a problem.

Your government is deciding how much to share your money with other people in your country, some of whom you believe are a threat to your survival or whose interests are antithetical to yours.

And so there is every incentive not to share this money. That is the system you have created, which allows for numerous ways of determining just how much money in taxes is actually supposed to be sent in, and you find all sorts of ways to make sure that the number you ultimately settle on is as small as possible.

In other words, your primary impulse in how you decide to share your money with the collective is based on your fundamental assumption of an antagonistic relationship between you and those who would ultimately receive it. You regard it as a penance, as a price you must pay, as a penalty, not as an action done for the welfare of all, for the benefit of all. Your system is infused from the very beginning with the idea that you need to protect your resources and that what you are handing over is a penalty, is a price that you must pay, but you do not want to give, you want to give as little as possible. The money that comes in, as we have said, is distributed according to the views of the very same people who do not want to give over money in the first place.

We can summarize by saying that you strive to give as little as possible, and those that could give the most are in the greatest position to reduce the amount they give, and those are the very same people who have the money to influence how that money is distributed so that it goes back to those who are least in need of it.

This is not a system that regards itself as a collective enterprise. No, this is a mean and nasty competition, and this is the system that you have set up. This is the combination of your political and legal systems working together to control the flow of money in a way that means that those who have the most money contribute the least, control the most, and benefit the most at the expense of the others.

❄

As we have already said, your relationship to money in various ways reflects your belief in separation, and so you allow some people to accumulate much more than others and then use it to further dictate how that money may be accumulated or distributed. Your banking system has been enormously corrosive in your society, and you have exerted much effort to grapple with the enormous power that the banking system wields politically and economically over you. You have these funny sayings like "no bank is too big to fail" or "too big to jail," and we do not fully understand your point. You speak as if banks could be jailed, when in fact that is not what is at stake.

What is at stake is the interweaving of the banks through your political system by means of their ability to influence the decisions of a host of actors in the political realm. This permits them to undertake all sorts of activities that go unregulated and unfettered, and you spend countless hours debating whether they should be able to do this or do that, and if so, what the ramifications are, yet you never address the very notion of a bank.

The idea of your banking system is that you wish to be able to store and accumulate wealth, to have the resources at your disposal in a place of safekeeping so that they may be distributed to others in an easy and timely manner. You do not ship lumps of gold. No, you have money stored in a bank, and thus a bank is first and foremost a storage system for your financial resources. It is also a conveyor, a communicator of your wealth to others, so that wealth may be transferred; it is an energy transfer system.

What happens when you allow the energy transfer system to play with the energy it is supposed to store and transfer? It loses that money. Why? Because the system is no longer invested in the retention and distribution of your money. No, it becomes interested in the playing with and growth of the money for itself, which is something separate from its original purpose. And this is what happens when you allow your banks to no longer be banks but something else, money-making machines that try to create money rather than store and distribute it. That's all it really boils down to, and you have many complicated designs for addressing this when the simple fact is that your banks should be storage and distribution centers for your money, not for the creation and growth of money.

Allowing them to be more allows their incentives to shift, and these banks are now interested in their own money creation, and this allows the egos of those working to step in and their incentives to shift. They are no longer aligned with your need to protect your money. They are more aligned with the creation of their own wealth, and what this means is that they take steps that put your money at risk. Your money is no longer their main goal. They don't care about your money. They care about *their* money, and you have permitted this by allowing a bank to be something other than a bank. It is as simple as that.

There is no other argument to be made but to have banks be banks if you want them to protect your money as a bank is designed to do, to store it and transfer it to others. You are not storing your money with banks when they have become something else. That is the risk you take. Yes, that is the risk when you allow the entity to have more than one mission, to have competing missions, and to seek out the mission that benefits itself because it is no longer in alignment with yours.

Do you not see how simple this could be if you would let it be that simple? If a bank is designed for the safekeeping of money, and it is not designed to make money on its own by investing that money and generating all sorts of new types of wealth and investments, then you should not allow it to do those things that are not a bank's job or task. That is when a bank is no longer a bank.

❊

Your structures, we have repeatedly said, and will repeat again, are a reflection of the collective consciousness. They are driven by a constant need to have more and more, far more than is necessary, to avoid the possibility that you might not have enough. So lack and excess are the two driving forces of your current approach to accumulating capital. You see this in the unequal distribution of income in your realm, where many people live very lavish, bountiful lives with the most elaborate and excessive homes and clothing, and jewelry and all sorts of accessories and gadgets, none of which actually bring them happiness, while so many of you have so little.

This is the problem: The amount that is required for you to feel happy, to feel the Light, to be at peace with yourself, to recognize that you are a Seed of Light, is not that great. It all depends on your ability to trust that you are taken care of, that you are loved, that you are so loved that nothing could ever really harm you, and you will always have your physical needs taken care of. But so few of you have this perspective.

So you are driven to gain and spend, gain and spend, and the constant gaining and spending is all built around the ego-based structures that dominate the collective consciousness. *I don't have enough, I am not enough, I need more to feel better about myself.* These are all substitutes for love. Money becomes your substitute for love, and as cliché as that sounds, this is the truth. It becomes your ego's substitute for love because of the underlying thoughts that you are not good enough, that you are not loved. This is what it means to be absorbed by the collective consciousness. Your capital structure is designed to feed that by allowing you to accumulate vast amounts of money and wealth and possessions, none of which will ultimately dispel that sense that you are not enough, as so many rich people already know, and yet they cannot find another way.

This means that so many of you do not have enough, have so little that it is difficult for you to perceive the world as full of Light and love, for you are too busy desperately trying to ensure the physical survival of your body. That is no small feat when you are deprived of all of the basic necessities to keep your physical self functioning.

We understand why this teaching might not seem to offer much hope, for it suggests that the very rich and powerful will have to alter their mindset, will have to seek to accumulate less so that there is more left for others. But it is not just at the feet of the rich, for those without vast amounts of money likewise seek to accumulate and hold on to much more than they actually need to compensate for the feelings of deprivation that they have suffered for so many years of their lives. This means that all of you are collectively responsible for the capital structure that exists today, as a reflection of your understanding of what it means to be human, separate from one another.

Ask yourself: Where do you not have enough and where do you have too much? And begin to see whether you can shift the collective consciousness ever so slightly, nudging it to a higher frequency, by saying to yourself, *I am enough, and I have enough.* Do you see the equation, between being and having? This is at the root of who you are in your mind; you equate being with having, and so ask yourself where you see yourself as less because you have less, and conversely, where you see yourself as more because you have more. For the structures in place are not just designed to ensure that you accumulate more wealth, but they are also designed to ensure that others do not, so that you can stand in contrast and opposition with them. *I have more than you, so I am more than you.* That is the message you have all embraced at the core, at the core of the collective consciousness. The structure of money that you have all agreed to—and in fact, many of you have aligned with it and seek to ensure its survival—is one that separates you all, so that some may have more and those that *have* more can say that they *are* more.

This is yet another way of laying claim to existence in this realm. To have money means to be money, to be energy, to be more in this physical universe. And that is of course false, and should be rejected. To have more money does not make you more, for you are all equal. You are all equal in the eyes of the Creator, you are slivers of the Creator, you are Seeds of Light, and all that you need is available to you. So you should shift the mind and ask yourself, *Where am I enough? Where do I have enough?* When you seek to have more, ask yourself, *Do I lack? Is this not enough?* And begin to examine, really, truly, and deeply examine, your motives for pursuing more money and more possessions. When you do, you may begin to see how you are pushed and prodded, urged along by the ego's demand, and that demand is one that says, *I am not enough.*

It is a lie. Don't believe it. You are more than enough. You are vaster than all of the oceans and skies. You are all of it. You are Seeds of Light.

11

SELF-INTEREST IN POLITICS

The issue of money reflects your deep preoccupation with self-interest, with the survival of your physical form. But self-interest also infuses the standards by which you evaluate each other and your so-called politicians, the ones who ostensibly represent you but so often seem to be seeking office for their own personal reasons. You struggle mightily with this issue of who can represent you, and who can do so in a way that isn't co-opted by their own needs and self-interest. Yet you do nothing to alter your minds, do nothing to train yourself to be different so that the minds that are operating in the places where you seek to root out corruption are in fact minds capable of foregoing self-interest.

Isn't it interesting how you continuously clamor for some sort of transparency and honest collaboration, and yet do you find those same qualities in your own life? Do you engage in the same behavior that you see on the national stage but in your own home, in your families, in the workplace? Yes, corruption is difficult to grapple with because it seems intrinsic to your system. Most of your news is about someone doing something in the name of self-interest that breaks a law or norm that was set down to ensure that there was a level playing field. Do you see the conundrum?

As a people, you are besotted with self-interest, and rather than eliminating your sense of self-interest by realizing the truth of who you are and that there is no self to protect, not really, you instead use your language to mitigate and ameliorate these tendencies to act out of self-interest, to elevate your needs over the needs of others. That is your flaw. Your flaw is that you elevate your needs over the needs of others because you perceive your needs to be somehow more important, and your own self more in need of protection than others, and this is in part because the others with whom you are co-creating reality regard *their* needs as more important, and therefore try to protect their needs.

While you engage in this constant struggle over your own needs, you attempt to elevate certain people to positions of power though they do not have any other mechanism for dealing with their own needs other than to elevate their own needs over the needs of others. Then you find that they do so in ways that are problematic. They run afoul of the rules you have set down to try to prevent people from doing so, and then you cry foul and claim that there is corruption. But you have all created each other—this is what you do when you are absorbed at the level of the collective consciousness and see your needs as the primary goal and the one thing that must be protected at all cost.

Your political system reflects this very same tendency to protect one's needs. Individual politicians protect their financial interest, their power, and then there are political parties, which are just groups of the same, who have banded together to protect their self-interest and needs. And so you cannot expect someone to represent you, to put your needs before their own, when your very consciousness is one that only protects one's own needs at the expense of others. Do you see the contradiction? Yet you demand of your politicians what you yourselves cannot achieve and in fact have done nothing to achieve. You ask of them the impossible.

All of you must begin to shift the collective consciousness, slowly, very slowly, so that you elevate the possibility of what can be. Can you see where you demand of someone else what you do not demand of your own self? That is the starting point. Yes, your political system will need some tremendous reconstruction over time, and this will happen, slowly but surely, as you continue to align with a higher possibility, a possibility in which the needs of all of you are already met, and you do not need to protect your own needs out of a sense of survivalism, because you can align to a different possibility. That is the abundance of this universe. The energy that is available to all of you now is tremendous, more so than in any other time in humanity's evolution, and so rather than watching the news and rejecting all of your politicians as being corrupt, recognize that they are mirroring an aspect of the collective consciousness that you all share. Your politicians are your creation, and your reflection.

You must create yourself in a different image. You must resurrect yourselves in a different image, drawing from the Christ Consciousness, and begin to embody a different subjectivity, a different consciousness, that does not see one's needs in isolation, does not seek to defend oneself through the same categories of identity that you have used to lay claim to your existence in this realm. Understand that you are loved and that you are taken care of, and begin to alter your relationship to reality, including your relationship to your political system.

Do not regard them all as crooks who need to be cast out. Do not look with indifference upon them. Look with the compassion of the Christ Consciousness that sees them as products of the collective consciousness in which you are all absorbed, and begin to align to the possibility that your politicians will themselves likewise align to a higher frequency, will begin to recognize their own divinity, their truth as Seeds of Light. For it is only when your politicians likewise claim their divinity, and the divinity of all of their constituents, that you will truly begin to see a shift in the nature of politics. It cannot be any other way.

The reality you experience is always in perfect alignment with the frequency of the consciousness that exists at that moment in time and space, and therefore you must align with a new reality, with a different consciousness, for the reality of your political system to change. Do not fall into old habits of judgment and criticism when you regard the political realm, and act as if it were separate from the spiritual world you inhabit. Do not use the spiritual realm to hide, as a sanctuary to which you can retreat from the political realm. They are all part of the same package, all part of this world that you all co-create. Instead, align with the possibility that the spiritual and the political will meld; that your politicians, like you, will discover their true nature as Seeds of Light and begin to operate differently.

❋

Your relationship to the political system that you currently have is the same relationship that you have with each other. But we wish to deepen this insofar as you find yourselves at the precipice, at the abyss, of an electoral system that is crumbling, of a political system that is coming apart at the seams. And while this may sound judgmental, again, it is not. This is merely a description of what is occurring for you, of what is occurring on the planet right now. Your system is breaking apart because the ego that has driven for so long is now coming up for inspection and release. The decadence and decay that you see is the release of a structure that can no longer hold sway.

But it does not go away easily. This is the nature of energy, of all energy, including all systems and structures that you have put into place. This energy does not wish to leave, does not wish to change shape. All energy tries to persist as itself. That is its nature. That is the nature of energy—to replicate itself.

So what does this energy wish to do? It replicates itself in all manner and creation, winding its ways through your systems, through your newspapers, your courts, your online presences. It is the energy of separation and judgment. That is all it is. And it is this energy that says, *You are not me, I am not you, and, ultimately, I am not loved.* That is the matrix of this energy; that is it at its core. However simplified this might seem, that is precisely what occurs with each and every one of you when you engage the ego. It is a fight to survive, and that survival depends on whether you believe that you are loved.

That is why your time and energy are spent constantly reiterating and sharing stories of good deeds and compassion and connection, and how the world would be better if you were all "this" way. But you are not all "this" way, you are not all this way all the time or even much of the time. No, that is not how you are. And so you resort to finding these examples that uplift you, that tell you that this is possible, that move you emotionally, but you never ever get to the core issue of feeling that you are not loved. That is the crux. If you felt loved, you would not engage in the behaviors that you do that lead to all sorts of difficulties in the realms of the world that you occupy. In every single instance, the issue can be boiled down to the single critical question: *Am I loved?* And almost always the answer that is driving the behavior is: *No, I am not loved.*

This is the thread that we are weaving throughout this book—how this question drives each and every one of your political, economic, legal, and cultural systems and structures so that you are constantly trying to answer the question *Am I loved?* with a *yes*, instead of a *no*.

That is currently what is occurring in your election, where so many people are attacking so many other people. You look at your candidates and say, *This person will make the world better for me*, or *This person will make the world worse for me*. You go on judging and evaluating each of those individuals against a standard that you cannot meet. Are these individuals perfect? Are they worthy of love? The answer is no and yes. That is true of all of you. And yes, many of the actions taken by them were rooted in that answer to their own question, *Am I loved?*, and the answer was invariably no. And so they take actions that reflect a need to avoid the feeling of that question, to avoid the crushing weight of the energy of not being loved. It all ultimately boils down to this very simple question—*Am I loved?*

❋

We have just explained that your political and legal system is built on this question of whether you are loved. Much of your collective response to all that occurs around you takes the form of this question, and it is really a question about self-preservation, for the fear that you are not loved, that you are not going to be loved or are not worthy of love, is crushing to you. It is a form of death, an annihilation, that says that you are less of a person. You are less here in this realm because you are not loved, in the forms of love that you currently perceive to be the forms of love available to you, which, as we have said in the past, are not the only forms of love available to you.[1]

That is your misperception—your limited view of the forms that that love can take. Instead, you ask, *Will you love me in this way, which I know and understand to be love because others have told me that it was love?* That is your way, and the result is that you evaluate your relationship with the world through this lens, through this question of what forms of love are available to you. And you regard your world according to whether your preservation, your self-preservation, is enhanced or diminished.

When you evaluate candidates for your highest office, for the President of the United States, to determine who will lead the country, and you speak in terms of what this person will do for the country, really you are saying what this person will do for you, for it is really about you personally in the end, what matters to you. And so you speak generally of how it would affect the economy or whether certain individuals will be allowed to stay or must go from your country, and this has everything to do with you deciding what is best for you.

Will you be safe? Will you be loved? Those are the same question for you, even though they are really not the same question. That is, again, the result of your misperception of the nature of love. But it means that you do not evaluate the selection of an individual to lead your country in a particular way without anything more than your own self-interest at heart. Yes, you do not evaluate what it would mean to everyone else, or whether the choice might have little effect at all on the world of some people. For many of you complain about how terrible the world is currently but your lives are actually quite abundant, and your minds simply focus on what is negative.

The choice of another President therefore requires you to be able to step outside your personal self-interest and take a broader view of the world around you. In fact, that broader view is the real you. It is the awareness that you are of all the possible ramifications of this choice. Your awareness of all those aspects of the world is who you really are—you are consciousness itself, occupying a body. But you end up identifying with this body and this limited mind, this portal into the physical realm, and think that is what you must defend. This is merely one way of interfacing with the physical realm. It can be a beautiful way of interfacing with the physical realm, but it is not the only way.

The way to broaden your perspective, to relate to the political realm in a manner that does not fall into the trap of self-preservation of your body and your way of life, is to dis-identify with that body and way of life and instead identify with *awareness*. You become aware of all the ways that the choice of President might impact others, and you must then take those aspects into account. For you begin to see that those lives are your life too, when you identify with awareness.

As you break away from the collective consciousness and the identity categories that you've used to establish and anchor your presence in this realm, you see that these are not the ways you need to claim existence as a living, breathing person. There are infinite ways of being, and then you can begin to appreciate all of them as simply that—as ways of being. They do not need to be defended as better or worse than one another, and therefore whatever your identifications might be do not need to be defended, either. Not in the sense that you need to protect that identity at the cost of all others. No, you can defend them all as viable ways of living. But that does not mean you even need the identity.

As you learn to be in a human body without identifications and the identities that you feel you must have to lay claim to existence in this realm, you become identified instead with awareness itself, with all of the possibilities for being in a human body that you see before you. You see that the lives of others who identify with different races, genders, ethnicities, sexualities, who come from other countries to join this one and start a different life, all of those people are part of your consciousness, and because you are awareness, they are part of you. You are them. And so the political choices you make will no longer be informed by, *What does this candidate do for me and my body?*, but rather *What does this candidate do generally? Does this candidate speak to all aspects of my awareness? Does this candidate seek to protect one set of identities, one way of being, over all others?* For that is the choice then you must choose—is this candidate interested in self-preservation, and the preservation of one way of being in this world, or is this candidate truly about allowing for the entire populace to live its life to its fullest potential? That is the only question you really need to ask. Everything else flows easily from that answer.

12

MONEY AS SPEECH

*O*ne of the many problems you face in your election of a
new President is that you have allowed a certain energy to pervade your discourse, and that energy is money. Your jurisprudence, your legal decisions, have equated the
energy of language and the energy of speech with the energy of
money, and is this is inaccurate. Both are part of the realm of
creation—they are energies of creation. You create with words
and speech, and you also create with money. We have spoken
of money as an energy of creation, as a capacity you have to
materialize in this realm through the medium of money.[1] But
it is not the same as speech, it is not, and not for the doctrinal
reasons that your Supreme Court has said.

This is a realm that Patrick understands as a lawyer, but we
wish to address it from our perspective, from the spiritual perspective, as a group of Light Beings who view this entire epi-
sode in human history with a different perspective.

Money and speech are not the same because of the simple fact that they are not the same type of energy. They operate differently. Money is energy that expects a return of energy. Language does not. Language creates without any requirement of an exchange or any giving back. You can provide words to another person, and this is done freely without any return, although they often do return words.

Say you want to buy some of food. You want a particular item in a shop, and you use your words to communicate with the other person. You indicate, I would like that item, and the person selects that particular items out of all the other items, and that means you are now ready to have that item. But wait, you must exchange something else, you must exchange money. That person is not giving you the item for free. No, the words do their work of navigating physical reality, but the exchange of form must take place. You both must exchange a certain type of energy. In exchange for the physical object, you are also giving energy in the form of a physical object, money, or at least a version of that physical object. It is energy in exchange for a physical object.

The use of words is free. There is an exchange, but it is free—free of the energy of form. You wish to compliment someone, and they may say thanks in return, but they do not have to. There is no obligation to give you those words. They may exchange other words with you, but the choice of words is free. You may pay someone to give a speech or to provide something to you with words, and then there is an obligation. You are paid to provide certain words, and to help in certain ways.

Consider if you paid a therapist who works with words, and you showed up and they decided they just wanted to talk you about the news or a TV show they watched last week, you would say, *I am not paying you for this.* You see, money is the energy that is used to reflect your intentions and the agreement is that the exchange of money provides you with a certain return in this realm, of something that you sought. You pay for a pastry, you don't get a car instead. You go to the showroom and purchase a car, they don't turn around and give you a pastry. You would think they were crazy if they did. Your use of money is the energy that says, *We are in agreement over an exchange of energy between us*, and that energy requires that you perform and return this energy in a particular way. It allows you control over your physical realm.

Another example. What if you paid the telephone company, and instead of getting cellular service, they sent you a gift basket? You would think, *That's a nice gift basket, but I didn't pay you for this. I paid for my phone, and I would like that service, please.* But if you tell someone you've met, "I love you," they don't have to say "I love you" back. If you write to someone, "I'd really like you to do this for me," they may say yes or they may so no. And how they speak to you with the words they use, will be dictated by something else. But if you were to hire someone, then the words they used and their response would be different. So you see how the energy works differently.

This confusion has generated the many problems of equating money with speech. You equate the use of money with being able to speak—the money that is necessary to have access to certain channels or media to be able to disseminate your speech, your words—and this has meant that you have allowed one type of energy, which always requires and commands a certain type of reciprocal exchange, to infiltrate that which does not require exchange. It is this fundamental difference that means that people give money and they say, *But this is just speech, I'm just showing support*, when in your realm, money always requires some sort of reciprocity or return. *I did not give you money so that you could ignore me. No, I gave money, and in return, there are expectations, expectations of a different sort.* Perhaps not the direct response like buying a car, or a pastry or a cell phone, but there is a reciprocity built into your concept of money.

And that is why your current system is so fraught, for those with money can therefore use the rhetoric of speech and support to exert influence. You all know this on some level, but your courts have twisted and contorted their own words to justify this conflation of money and language in ways that do not reflect how those two types of energy actually work.

13

CORRUPTION IN POLITICS

Your conflation of speech with money is at the core of one of your great concerns: corruption. Corruption is something that you are all preoccupied with in your worlds of economics, politics, and law. You worry about corruption in politicians, and many of you view them all as corrupt. You worry about Wall Street and how they are corrupt and do things to make money that cost the rest of the country greatly. You worry about corruption in the legal system, where you think of most lawyers as corrupt, and occasionally judges, particularly judges who do not rule in ways that seem to benefit your position.

Examine your relationship to corruption and why it bothers you to see it on a systemic level. Ask yourself why you find corruption so unnerving. What does it say or mean to you?

That is the fundamental starting point for the Christ Consciousness to enter and articulate a new vision and new relationship to these three realms, for it is this concept of corruption that is at the core of your concerns. You are constantly arguing about ways to alter that system, and how someone new is going to valiantly stride in and take over and lift you all out of the corrupt mess you find yourself in. But that is not the case, that is not the case, as you have seen in the eight years where your President Obama, a very sincere and well-meaning man, came in with the idea of building consensus only to find that he could accomplish or do little that he wanted because everyone was invested in their own power.

Your concern is often around corruption and the accumulation of resources, that people do things to gain power or money. This is, for you, the source of corruption. Politicians do what they do to ensure they stay in office and make sure others do not get into office or remain in office, and people working on Wall Street and lawyers work to ensure that they make money and others do not, regardless of the effects on others or whether their clients are actually in the right. And so you equate the accumulation of power and resources with corruption. The underlying belief is that there is a way to be that is not corrupt, there is a right way to be, and it is not a way that would lead to actions that are designed to protect one's self-interest at the expense of the whole.

Your instinct is right—there is a way—but to get there you must first understand your relationship to corruption, your fear of corruption, and what corruption means. Otherwise, any attempt to transform your society will ultimately fail, will ultimately return to the same structures that are already in place and which have dominated you for centuries.

We began by pointing to your relationship to corruption. It bothers you. It invokes a visceral response. It causes you great angst, and you rail against corruption. You see it as an abomination, as a distortion, as somehow a bending of truth. And we ask you to first examine why this might bother you so deeply. This is not to suggest that this is okay or that corruption is good; we are not in the realm of judgment.

Understand what your emotional relationship to corruption is and why it might upset you so. When you delve beneath the surface, corruption upsets you because it raises an existential, even an ontological, question of what it means to receive love. And that question is tied to a belief in the purity and honesty of love. Love given honestly and authentically is one of the most powerful forces there is. But you can understand that sense of betrayal and deceit when love is found to be a ruse or a lie, that it is nothing but trickery. That sense of betrayal is very deep. Many have suffered massive emotional wounds as a result of that trickery, when love turns out to have been a mirage. Yes, that is painful.

What would it mean to find out that your mother never really loved you or that your father never really wanted to conceive you, that you were not truly and entirely loved by your spouse? What would it mean to find out the person who devoted themselves to you in fact lied, that it was a mere ruse to get your money or something like that? You would feel such a sting, because at the root of your entire subjectivity, at the root of the collective consciousness, is this profound belief that you are not loved, that you are not lovable, and thus you mistrust. You mistrust quite easily, far more easily than you love. And the result is that you are on constant vigilance for the breakdown of love, for the betrayal and corruption of what you once believed in.

Do you see how you are already setting the stage for corruption at a societal level? You are already in a state of constant
mistrust with those around you, and therefore you have far less
belief in those who purport to have your interests at heart but
are not professing love, nothing so grand as love, but merely to
represent you in the name of justice or what is right, or in the
name of a nation, such as in the preservation of a national identity. Do you see that what binds you to all those who purport
to represent you is something even less powerful, less tangible
than love itself? And because none of you trust, because you
believe that you are not loved, you must defend yourself, you
must protect yourself against the inevitable specter of not being loved, of the core wound you might say, that resides in the
center of all of you.

Now, you know this is not true. We have explained your true
nature as Seeds of Light, but we will not belabor that. Our teachings on this point may be read elsewhere.[1] But the fact remains
that this core concern with lovability structures your relationship to the entire social stratum. Your lack of trust and lack of a
true and authentic relationship to each other leads to political
relationships that are not bound by anything powerful. No, they
are bound by the individual's concern for self-interest. *You will
represent my self-interest*, and yet this elected person's interests
may be different from yours, or those interests may require something else than what your interests require. So you are always
suspicious that those interests, the interests of the representative,
the interests of those supposedly working on the side of justice,
are actually working on behalf of self-interest—their self-interest.

This is your fundamental relationship to corruption. It is the
symptom of your fear of unlovability being born out. By seeing

others as interested in their self-preservation and ferreting it out, you are really protecting your own sense of self-interest, and projecting outward, to the mirror that stands before you, your own concerns with self-interest.

Your politicians, and your Wall Street bankers, and your lawyers and judges are really no different. There is nothing about the system that purports to be any different. You hold corruption up as an idea precisely because you need something to protect against self-interest. The very existence, for example, of all sorts of ethical rules that govern your behavior is the perfect evidence of how you have behaved in ways that are designed to protect your self-interest over the collective interest. Yes, you would not have ethics rules in place if you did not have to worry about people actually elevating their own interests over the interests of those they purport to serve. Your judges and lawyers would be bound by their own sense of what is right, and the higher good of the justice system. The same would be true of politicians. Your fear of corruption is really your fear of unlovability at the core of who you are, and this is played out in the major systems of your society.

We will explore later how to approach this corruption, and what it would look like if this were not your focus, and what a society not built on separation, but on the Christ Consciousness, would look like.

14

DEMOCRATIC REPRESENTATION

*W*e have explained that you are driven primarily by this concern about unlovability, as expressed through the focus on the topic of corruption. We do not disagree with the concern you have with corruption. We are not attempting to tell you that corruption is to be ignored. Rather, as it emerges in your social structure, your relationship to it provides you the path to correcting it. For that is what corruption is—energy in need of correction. It is misguided. It is not aligned with what it should be aligned with. This is energy as the product of fear, of survival-based fear. That is all.

Now, this allows us to proceed to a different topic. We wish to speak of democracy, and what the term means to you and how you relate to it. For as a word, it contains energy, and you have spent much of your energy in advancing this particular type of system, this particular way of government, of organizing yourselves collectively. You do this in small ways, and in large ways, and we applaud its foundation in the sense that you believe that democracy is about ensuring that all of you have the same access. It is built on egalitarian principles, and this we applaud, just as we applaud you as Seeds of Light who are equal in the eyes of the Creator.

You wish to spread a system that reflects egalitarianism. The very idea of your system is that all people should be represented equally, and, as we have said, this conflicts with your internal struggle for self-preservation, so that those chosen to do this work on your behalf often struggle with their own self-preservation. Whom do they represent? They represent themselves and others who can ensure that they continue to represent. Your democracy is built on the capacity to be able to tell those who represent you say that you no longer wish for them to represent you, and this is a powerful choice. This is a powerful way of co-creating each other, which allows you to recreate something anew. A new person may be installed as your elected leader or representative, and this occurs in small ways at local levels and at your national level as well. The system is the same. You may choose to say, *You no longer represent me.*

But you may be divided in your wishes. Some may want to keep this representative, and some might not. At this point, your ability to sway the person to quit the job or your power to put someone else in office is no longer equal. Some of you will have more power than others to make this choice. Some of you will wield more influence, and the egalitarian principle that you sought to instill is no longer operative. No, a shift in influence has taken place. And this happens all the time in your system. The shift in influence constantly betrays the egalitarian principle that you sought to achieve. A laudable effort to be sure, but it fails nonetheless, not because of lack of trying but because inevitably the concern for self-preservation drives some to influence more than others. So your elected officials must then make choices about whose influence matters more. Those of you who seek to elect a representative are now divided, for your views do not align with one another's views as to who is the right candidate. Some will want one candidate and others another, and your interests are no longer aligned.

You often speak in rhetorical terms about all the things that you want. You want change, you want transparency, you want honesty. But these are all a reflection of the original concern with corruption and unlovability. The source of this confusion stems from the ways in which you use language and money. For there is suddenly alignment between those who are guided by self-interest and those who are willing to provide money and not just words. Yes, those willing to provide money and not just words of support are providing an energy (money) that aligns more directly with the energy of self-preservation of the candidate. The candidate then feels that they are in an exchange. They may never really admit to that, they may not believe that there is a so-called *quid pro quo*, but they are in the realm of monetary exchange and thus remain more tied to those who *ensure* their self-preservation than to those who simply support with their words or with a vote. That egalitarian principle in your democracy has shifted, and has shifted again along two types of energy, from language to money. And so the balance of influence has shifted as well.

What does this mean for the Christ Consciousness? It means you must understand how and why those in office say certain things and do other things. For they speak a language that you all aspire to and yet are driven by the concerns of self-preservation, and this means that the influence, who they are aligned with, also changes. They do not and cannot represent you equally, because they are aligned more with others who can provide them with an energy (money) necessary to their survival.

What does the Christ Consciousness do here?

You do not need to "do" anything. From the perspective of the Christ Consciousness, you are merely witnessing how the system works and altering your relationship to it. Your relationship to that system is what you focus on—not necessarily any specific actions. You will relate to it differently because you will see it through the eyes of the Creator, as the product of a series of misguided steps taken by Seeds of Light who are absorbed by the collective consciousness.

In other words, you simply recognize that they are driven by their self-preservation and you forgive them. You forgive them the way you forgive anyone who has forgotten their true nature and acted out of ego. That it takes place at a systemic level makes no difference. The energy that you put out in response— to condemn, vilify, and to cast out—is equally resonant with the collective consciousness, and is part of the problem. You must begin to release your anger toward a system that you regard as flawed and corrupt, and which does indeed respond to an imbalance of influence through money. Anger will do nothing to alter that system. Forgiveness will begin to shift your relationship to it.[1]

15

WARMONGERING

*T*he mirroring of your internal state at the national political level is further reflected in the way that you relate to the rest of the world, and in particular, your commitment to war. Your penchant for war leads the United States to act as a type of global police officer who patrols the world in an effort to ensure that its vision of global peace is adopted and reinforced. The United States relates to the rest of the world in terms of its supposed extraordinariness and uniqueness and then proposes to set itself up an arbiter of how the world is to be. And this is to be applauded on one level, for the United States is exceptional in many respects with regard to its foundational efforts and, in particular, its original commitment to freedom of speech and to a certain type of equality. That the United States has not lived up to its original foundation is not at issue here; we can speak at great lengths about the history of slavery in this country, the legacy of discrimination, and the problems that beset its current state. But our concern here is its effort on a global level to set itself up as the patrolman, as the entity that enforces and keeps others in check.

This is an important topic because the way your nation constructs itself in relationship to the world has a bearing on how your nation treats its own citizens. For you are in some ways all conscripted into a machinery of war, a machinery of policing on a global scale, and this plays out in the engine of war that is your material industrial complex, and the vast resources that you devote to this entity, to this aspect of your government. The resources are far more vast than your average citizen realizes, and the tendrils of power that extend between the military and the government are many. In fact, it would not be an exaggeration to say that they are not even separate entities. The military and the executive branches in your nation are so intertwined that there is no difference. You elect individuals who are going to lead, as a commander in chief, the military industrial complex around the world to ensure that other countries behave a certain way. The effect is to reduce the resources that are available internally for the consumption of the citizenry. The populace has many needs and yet those resources are channeled to the exterior in the form of military interventions elsewhere. You ask yourself, *Why is this necessary?* And of course, the inevitable answer is that this is necessary to protect yourselves, protect your way of life, and because no one else will do it.

That of course is not true. That is not true at all.

❊

And this same relationship of separation sets up an us vs. them relationship between you and the rest of the world, so that you are at war with the rest of the world, and the rest of the world is a threat, an intruder. And you have seen this play out most recently in the way that you handle anyone who wishes to join your nation, who wishes to come in and through the borders, the geographic lines that you have arbitrarily carved up in the earth, in Mother Gaia, and which have no meaning for her other than that you have agreed to them.

Yes, the nation's boundaries are nothing more than an agreement, and yet the world's population is continually testing those boundaries, pushing and showing that they are not there for any reason but to protect the interest of the nation, or so it believes. But the nation does not need to be protected, it does not need to defend itself in the way that you think it does. The immigrant or outsider is not the enemy. And you will say, *But they attacked us, they harmed us. We must keep them out.* And this is the same mechanism that you use to jail people: to isolate them. You draw up walls and barriers and close ports and tell people, *You may not enter. You must stay out.* And this is the relationship you have with yourself, internally, as a nation. It is all separation writ large.

So what is the way forward? Recognize that your lines, the boundaries of what you call a nation, are just a creation in language. They are an agreement, backed by power, backed by military might to enforce that agreement, and there is nothing about it that is essential to your wellbeing or existence. No, there is nothing essential about it. You could very easily open the borders and allow people to move about, and you would have the same problems as you do now. Those are the problems born of separation, and so drawing another boundary will not solve the problem. You would face the same concerns of someone coming in and bombing you because of some act you've done in the past as a nation, and yet the barriers you impose do little to resolve that karma.

Did the United States do something to another nation that caused it great harm, and those citizens now want to harm the United States in return? Yes, and so the original trauma, the original wound is there, still to be healed. But you don't heal. You continue to fight and you continue to inflict pain through wars and other military inventions, and you create the source of the backlash against you. And so you can and should open your borders. But remember that whatever follows is not the result of the open borders. It is the result of your minds collectively operating through separation, through fear and self-interest and self-preservation and the corruption that comes from the fear that you are not enough, that you are not loved, and therefore you must take, you must control, and you must defend and protect yourself. The barriers, the arbitrary barriers of your nation, do nothing to prevent that. They are just another manifestation of the same collective consciousness rooted in separation. Whatever harms that ensue cannot be solved with barriers, with expulsion—what you call deportation. They can only be solved through the Christ Consciousness that sees them as part of a global whole, a global family, that needs to be loved and made to belong.

16

THE DEVALUATION OF LIFE

We have been elaborating on how your society is built entirely on separation, and the many ways that you continue to permit separation to occur. How are you going to restructure your society in a way that allows for everyone to be included? That is the purpose of your being here: to include everyone, including those you don't want to include. Why do you not want to include them? They show you where you are in judgment.

We have already discussed how few topics divide you more than abortion and the way it elicits judgment from you. What additional guidance can we give you? We have already said that this is your free will. You are entitled to not carry the child to term, to not raise the child. But you are terminating the life stream. There is life flowing through you at the moment of conception. There is nothing more to discuss. The fact that it is not viable, is way too small to survive, does not matter. There is life.

That is not the issue. You condemn it, but you are all terminating life all the time. You're killing animals, killing plants, doing things that end the flow of life in this world. That is what you do. You kill animals and eat them. You kill plants, step on them, and eat them; you kill bugs. You end life all the time. You also end life all the time with the way you cut each other off and say, *I don't want you, I don't want* you. *I don't want that person in my life. No, no, no.* Ending life. You shut down life.

You do not accept killing other people, except if it is war. You tell yourselves, *Now we can kill each other, because we have decided that we are going to call this* war, *because we are protecting ourselves.* And then you kill. Why is it that two people in the street killing each other are not at war? Because you've decided that they are not nations. Another word, another label. Why not let five people call themselves a nation? They can say they are at war. You call those *gangs.* There is no difference. This is just a choice of words to group people. There is really no difference. When you kill an animal, kill a person, or kill a plant, you end life. When you terminate a pregnancy, you end life. It's as simple as that. You have simply chosen to end some forms of life. That is your free will.

Christians among you say that this is a sin, and that you're going to hell, that God condemns you. Does God condemn you? No, but there are karmic consequences. What do we mean? Perhaps there were lessons for you to learn. Perhaps that child was going to contribute to the world in a way that you could never have anticipated, and you had an important role in this, but you terminated that life stream. That was your choice. That is free will. Did you know what was going to happen with that child? No, you didn't. You couldn't possibly. But you chose not to allow that life to happen, you chose a different way, so you have aligned with a different experience of life.

Will that life stream come in another way? Yes, it will, yes it will. It will choose another way to come in.

✻

We have already told you that it is a mistake to conflate the karmic consequences of an abortion with the wrath or judgment of God. There is no difference between any act where you end life, where you end life as the flow of energy of creation in and through the living body of some other entity, and that is why it is not what you call a cardinal sin to commit an abortion or kill a cow for food or chop down trees for buildings or all the other ways in which you discontinue life.

Now, there are serious consequences to ending a human life, and Patrick is wondering whether this means that there's no difference between the murder of an individual and an abortion.

We understand the difficulty in contemplating this, and on one level, there is no difference. There are karmic consequences to both. But understand that once a person is living their own life, fulfilling their soul mission, there is *nothing* you can do to justify ending their life stream. The end of their life stream must come of its own accord. You cannot simply choose for them, whether that is murder or even just determining that it would be better if they were to be euthanized. No, they are a separate being at that point insofar as they and you view each other as separate in time and space.

That is the difference. For when the mother is still carrying the small seedling that will become a separate entity, that child is not yet separate, not yet on its own soul path. You can terminate the life, and there are karmic consequences because the effects that child would have had on the mother's life stream will be unknown to you. And by "karmic consequences," we simply mean that the impact of this child's life on the mother and the world in general will now be unknown to you. Who knows what the mother's life and other people's lives would have been like if that child had been born? But until that point: It is the mother's choice to carry the child to term, to have this life grow and expand within her, for it is part of her own life stream. It is her own body, contained by the soul, that experiences this.

Does it not sound like viability would be the line? As if to say, if the child could be separate, then it would be okay? And we say that this is not relevant to the karmic consequences. No, it is not relevant to what the karmic consequences are, for the child, until birthed, is part of the mother; it is an entity and as much a part of the mother as any other part of the mother, and so it is the mother's free will that guides. Yes, she may be more aware of the possibilities of the karmic consequences to her the closer the child is to birth. At this point, the reality that she is about to create another life stream is fully impressed upon her, and then she has to contemplate the meaning of the impact on her if she aborts the child. But this is different from the karmic consequences of ending another life that is wholly outside of your own. Those involve the repercussions in your society, the numerous effects of this person's loss on others, and the harm to the person's own life path and soul's evolution for having ended another Seed of Light's life. The damage to your soul from ending another Seed of Light's life is enormous.

❉

In truth, in addressing this controversial topic, we are speaking about the ways in which you measure and value life in your society, and what a society built on the Christ Consciousness would do to measure the value of life. You know that this is an easy answer: The measure of life is always the same. It is always the same value; there is no measuring of the value of life. It is simple: It is valuable. That is it, and yet you have a society built on valuing life in ways that does very little to actually promote life. No, you do not promote life. You promote death in so many ways. You promote smallness and weakness and obsolescence, and you promote the limitation of each other.

What would a new society look like? This would require reform at all levels; every aspect of your society would need to be rethought in ways that reflect what it means *not* to view each other as separate, *not* to view each other as an instance of another being separate and apart, along the axes of space and time. We will provide examples of what that society would look like as we continue to diagnose and identify the various structures in your society that have continued to reflect your profound belief in separation and are now undergoing massive decay and revision. This is inevitable. Do not despair. This is all part of the change that must occur for all of you to ascend into becoming the Seeds of Light that you truly are, and not the limited versions of yourself that you have contented yourself with being for millennia. Now is the time for the Christ Consciousness to slowly begin to rise and lift up aspects of your society that you had left untouched.

This may be shocking and unnerving for many of you, for we will begin to show you a wholly different way to live life, and a wholly different way to *promote* life. For that is what your new society must do: It must promote life, not acquiescence to a model that has outlived its purpose and is no longer valid.

You do not always evaluate and measure life consistently. No, you do not. You put people in prison, you contain them, and when they leave they are never allowed to be what they are supposed to be. You have effectively ended their lives. You have trapped them in ways that you could not imagine unless you had been through it yourself. You impose a form of death on them by preventing them from being and becoming what they are supposed to be. This is what you do to so many, many people. You have imposed a form of death on them.

Why do you do this? You are afraid of their actions and so you regard them as separate from you. You do not see your response to imprisoning them as actually killing off portions of yourselves. You contain them until you are safe, safe from those people, *safe from those people that we don't want*. That is what you believe. This is incorrect. You have just chosen to kill a portion of yourself.

In a new society, you cannot do this; you cannot commit the karmic killing off of a portion of yourself. With abortion, you can allow people to do this. This is a choice; this is free will. You cannot condemn the mother, but you can find ways of supporting her. Why do expectant mothers end their pregnancies? Why do they not carry a pregnancy to term? They could have numerous reasons, and you are there to support them, and to allow them to make this decision, so that it is truly one of free will, and not one of fear. What would a culture that looks to sustain and promote life look life?

It would not look like this current system. You would not put people in prison, you would provide them with support so they don't choose to terminate life because they don't believe they have the means to survive. Some people are going to go ahead and have abortions. That is okay. That is not a sin. Understand that for many women the decision is based on their understanding of who they think they are and the support they have and why they are having a child and what it would mean to them.

So a woman makes a decision based on a limited understanding of who she is and what she can deal with and the impact that this child's life will have on her. We do not judge her. This is her free will to choose her path. Do not condemn her. Let her choose until the moment of birth. At that point, what support is there for her in this world? That is the question you must ask yourself. It is not a question of protecting the child from being aborted. It is a question of providing the mother and the child with the support that they need for life in this world.

17

CORPORATE CONTROL OF FOOD

*W*e are speaking of how you value life, and as part of that, we wish to address something fundamental in your realm: the issue of food. You often do not think about food except to the extent that you are hungry, except to the extent that you wish to be made to feel good. And that is okay. It is an enormous pleasure to be able to feed the human form, to give the physical body its nourishment in the form of physical energy. This is an amazing pleasure, one that you should enjoy. It is a gift of the human body.

But do not ignore the fact that you are moving toward a crisis in your realm, a crisis that few of you seem to be paying much attention to. This sounds like we're lecturing, Patrick is saying, and yes, we understand that we are trying to impress upon you an important aspect of your realm, so fundamental to the physical wellbeing of the human form, yet you seem to ignore it. Food is a major aspect of your life, without which you would simply not survive as humans. And yet you do little to protect yourselves from all the ways that your food system is being taken over by the same corporate interests that have taken over your political system.

Do you think this is happenstance? Do you think is that is just chance? No, the control of your political system and the control of your food system by the same corporate structure is an example of how the most fundamental aspects of your society are being dominated by a legal fiction that you have created to accumulate wealth. There is something entirely perverse about the nature of a system that says, *We will allow this entity, this creation of our own making, fashioned out of words, to amass such control and power over the most fundamental of our needs, the very building block of life.* As if to say, *Yes, we will cede that control to you, and then you can dictate to us the terms under which we eat.*

For this is happening at all levels, from the foods that are grown and packaged to how you raise animals as livestock for your consumption. All of it is now under the control of a select group of companies who can tell you what to eat. This is madness, we say, and it is incumbent upon all of you to take a stand and raise your consciousness around the types of foods that you consume and under what circumstances. You have choices, and this is how you can begin to align to another option, to begin to call in a different frequency for your food. We have already said that you are capable of bending time and space by aligning yourself with new possibilities, and that you can begin to call a different system into being.[1] We have already shown you this in another context, and we will do so again here.

What is the way to call in a new food system? Inform yourselves and ask for greater and greater possibilities. Here is a verbal formula for you to consider: *What I am about to take into me will become me, and so I ask for the food the highest vibration to being to reach me so that I may be elevated in my physical form.* Yes, that is what you must do: Invite in a higher possibility. A higher frequency of food is always available to you. You may find that certain foods no longer appeal, and that you continue to align to a higher frequency of food. You may find that old places no longer appeal to you or that new food items come to you. Simply be open to the possibility that other food is available to you, and that your ability to effectuate change comes from the choices you make.

What about nature? Is there more you'd like to share about our relationship to food, the environment, and nature?

This is not a book about your relationship to the natural world. We have already spoken of the need to not project your consciousness onto nature,[2] and the ways in which you treat the environment and the planet without any regard for its status as a living entity.

You do not understand what it is you are doing with your seeds and with your industrial approaches to livestock. You do not understand the nature of animal consciousness at all, and so you do all sorts of things that inflict pain and suffering, and then you also just abandon animals altogether, without actually understanding how they regard the use of their byproducts and bodies for your sustenance. You do not understand the consciousness of the natural world at all; this is beyond your current consciousness.[3] Very few of you have been able to really connect with the natural world. This is not the book for that topic.

We are here to help you to understand how to relate to each other individually, to understand your own nature, to understand your nature in relationship to each other and to build a society. That you do not understand the natural world certainly influences your society's structures, and it speaks to how you waste and destroy without knowing what you do. But you are not ready to fully contemplate the nature of consciousness beyond the human form. And so we do not venture in this area yet. Someday, perhaps, as humanity continues to grow.

18

ELECTION REFORM

We wish to speak of your voting system, and how you choose others, and we've already spoken about how your system is not designed to choose the candidates that the public wants. No, the system is designed to choose the candidates that those in power want, and this is done by arranging how the votes are partitioned and allocated to the candidates you choose. You have this system called an "electoral college," which allows for certain votes to be aggregated in certain ways, and this permits you to elect people in ways that do not conform to what the actual majority of people want. Why do you do this? You do this because your elites always fear the public and what the public will do. What does this have to do with the arrival of the Christ Consciousness in this realm, and how does it affect the new society we are outlining? It reflects the ways that you believe, and much of your system is built on, the allocation of power by a few to control many other people.

Your system is built on a collective consciousness in which very few actually wield power, and the rest of you are to follow, and we have said that this appears in many contexts.

Voting is simply another example of the ways in which your system tells you that you can make choices when in fact those in power have already made the choices for you. And so you have to approach these issues differently. You can and should exercise the choices you make, but how many of you continue to champion the changes that would be necessary to your system's survival after you have cast your vote? No one does. This issue disappears, and then it returns in the next cycle. You never alter your system in any meaningful way, to ensure that you are actually given a voice. For your vote is an expression of energy. It is an expression of energy that supports another person and is attempting to alter the current way your society operates—and as such, it is important for you to ensure that your energy is being used in the way you choose.

Yet if that energy has nowhere to go because the system is designed in a manner that contains that energy rather than letting it flow, you must alter the system and approach it differently. For again, you have ostensibly built a society that says your needs are being represented by another. Then, as we have said, those needs are not met, not represented, because of the self-interest of the politician and the needs of the corporations, who are able to exercise influence through the accumulation and donation of money. And so your energy, the energy of the vote, is lost.

So what do you do? How do you change things? You cannot continue to operate in the same manner. You must choose to alter the ways those systems are operating, and this means you must take meaningful action in the ways that are available to you within the collective consciousness. How many of you continue to ask for changes to the electoral system when the election passes? If you do not, then you have acquiesced, you have gone into alignment with the system as it currently stands. And then you complain about the system the next time an election comes around.

But you can operate at the level of the collective consciousness *and* begin to articulate the changes that are necessary. Remain steadfast in your commitment to seeing that change. You can work at the level of frequency, at the level of consciousness, to see changes made. When you cast a vote, always remember that your vote is a piece of energy, a collective drop of energy that goes into the rest of the system, and you can begin to articulate a new meaning for that vote. As you vote, and you should vote, say, *May my vote alter and raise the frequency of this system, so that necessary change may occur.* Hold that intention as you vote and see what happens. You can begin to alter the system, ever so slightly, almost imperceptibly, and then continue with your efforts to see change made through the mechanisms you already know.

19

NATIONALISM

*I*t is not only your individual systems—political, economic, social, and legal—that are undergoing massive change, but also your global consciousness. On a global scale, all of the structures and agreements that you have had in place and that have governed your relationships with each other are beginning to break. They are beginning to unwind and stretch and come undone. This is expected; this is planned. This is already written. Do not fear what is coming, for that will make the arrival of what is to come even more difficult for you.

Understand that the bonds that have held you together are ones rooted in a different paradigm, a different notion of what it means to be human. And so you have constructed yourselves in numerous ways according to what you believed you needed to be kept alive, and to thrive in what seems like a difficult and hostile realm. We understand and appreciate this. We know how difficult it can be to be in a human body, and how you have organized your lives to make the best of it.

There is obviously great joy in the human form, so much pleasure to be had, but you also deal with great pain, and you organize yourselves in order to mitigate that pain. But the assumption is that pain is necessary. Yes, that is your primary assumption—that pain is necessary to human existence. Pain is a product of the mind. It is a product of your own mind's perception of what occurs to you and is just a construct of the collective consciousness that binds you all. What you need to do is alter how you relate to what is occurring around you, what you are manifesting, for this will alter how you experience it. It will no longer be pain even if the circumstances themselves have not changed form. You will see something else.

What is happening is the rearrangement of form in your realm, around individuals and the collective identities to which you remain attached and beholden. You are organized by cities and by states or regions or provinces and then by countries and then the globe. Do you see that at each stage you add a few more people and that becomes a group, and you identify a common trait where you draw a boundary and say, *This is us, and that is not us*. This is separation.

You are just at the beginning, but what is occurring now is the unfolding of a paradigm of relating to each other where those structures, those political structures in particular, are beginning to unwind and come apart. Something new will replace them, but not in your lifetime, not in the lifetime of most the readers of these words. That is the reality. Your physical form will pass, and you will return to non-form, and you will experience a new reality, and this reality on the earth will continue to unfold with the consciousness of those who remain embodied.

Do not fear; do not fret. You are helping to create a new realm, and what you must do now is assist in relinquishing the old. Yes, this is what you must do with all of your systems. You must begin to usher in new systems that replace those new ones. They will not be the perfect form. No, they will not be the ultimate replacement. Do not fear. You are simply paving the way for greater and greater transformation as new and more systems are replaced faster and faster each time, until you arrive at the ultimate emancipation from separation.

That emancipation is not happening just yet. What you must do, however, is recognize that what is occurring now is not the end of the world. No, it is not the end of the world. It is the upheaval that occurs as systems of energy that do not wish to be changed are attempting to rebirth themselves again and again, even more strongly. They try to take on a stronger presence and more energy to maintain their foothold in this realm. So nations are seemingly embattled and fighting harder and harder to maintain their collective unity and identity, but they are all coming apart at the seams. Countries are resorting to old tactics to try to outdo other countries and nations. And countries are using more and more tools that are available to them to undermine each other.

This is happening because the nation itself as a construct will eventually give way to a global identity. There will be no nations. That is just a construct that you have all used for millennia. You have had empires for millennia, and that is not going to be the way of the future. No, it is not. What will be the way of the future is *unity*.

And so what you must do is align, consistently align, with the new, with a higher possibility for your system, and ask, *What would a more inclusive system look like?* For that is the basic principle: inclusivity as you move toward unity. It means dropping the barriers that you use to divide between "us" and "them." And as you ask what a more inclusive system would look like, other aspects of what you have created will come up for review. You will begin to ask, *Why do we have this system in place, and why do we keep these people out, and how do we require that these people in the system act in this manner?* These are the questions you will ask, and each time, ask yourself, *What would something more inclusive look like?*

Open yourself to the possibility of something you have not considered before, and ask for that to be presented. Open to the new, to the unimagined, and innovation will arrive. That is what you must do. So as you watch your systems—financial, economical, political, judicial, etc.—and you see all of the terror and horror and frustration and pain emerging, and it is so powerful, ask yourselves, *What would a more inclusive, just, and loving system look like?* Yes, you can add more words, but the importance is always to focus on unity, on inclusivity, and to be open to what is new, what you have not yet invented or seen. That will allow you to align with possibilities that have not been experienced in this realm and which will allow for the new to arrive, so that eventually, one day, there will be unity on this planet.

20

POLITICAL PARTISANSHIP

*Y*our political system and its two parties is the primary
and most obvious way in which you replicate the collective consciousness. Yes, you replicate it by forming
two parties, and these you each separate from the other. You
define yourselves according to a binary, which, as we have explained, is the classic means of structuring the ego.[1]

So you know exactly what we mean when we say that as you
define yourselves by one party, and identify as that party, you
are defining yourself in opposition to another party. Those operative identities then take over and take on lives of their own,
controlling what and how you look at the issues that affect
you—and no longer through questions like *How does this affect
all of us?* or *How does this relate to fear or love?* or *How is this inclusive or exclusive?* No, the questions become: *Does this advance
our party?* or *Does this advance our position of power vis-à-vis the
other party?* Occasionally, other, smaller parties try to break up

this binary, but your system cannot accommodate them; they are merely influences at the fringes of the majority of voters. It is the binary that is the problem, and those two parties become the framework, and they are a framework of separation.

You cannot ever achieve a system of government built on unity when you are built upon an identification between two parties. There will be no true unity. None at all. There will always be a back-and-forth between these two groups, in some way, because that is how you have organized yourselves. Again, there is no way for third parties that come along to disrupt this structure, for they cannot address the fact that this is question of how your *minds* are structured.

So how should you relate to them, in order to change this? You do not relate to the parties. You begin to *dis-identify* with the parties. That is the only way you can begin to undermine the two-party system. Again, you are not going to solve this problem in your lifetime, so understand that the task that you are undertaking here is not going to achieve the results that you would hope for. You are aligning yourselves with a possibility, with another frequency, that will eventually come into manifestation when the collective itself comes to align with this possibility. That is not happening any time soon.

What you must do is adopt and embrace the frequency of unity, and continue to endorse and ask for those people who are in office to align with unity. Do not align with them because they have embraced a party label. That is the first step. You must see the positions that are staked out and align with the possibility of inclusiveness and unity at all times.

Does this position bring us toward love or toward fear? That is the basic question you must always ask, and then from there, the answer will be clear where you head toward inclusiveness and unity, and where you head toward exclusiveness and separation. But the attitude you cannot take is one in which you continue to embrace a party identification, and see yourself in opposition to those in the other party, and then judge and vilify the other party for their position.

Nor can you simply exit and write off as irrelevant the entire political system. No, you must continue to align to the possibility that these people will begin to understand their true nature and begin to see themselves in each other, and try to bring forth the fullness of who they are. That is, they will come to see themselves as divine Seeds of Light. This is what you must do, but you do not when you condemn them for belonging to the other party, or condemn them because they do not embrace your positions. Instead, you can rely on the power of forgiveness and the power to bend time and space by standing in the position of those who would see unity and inclusion. You stand for the possibility that those who cannot yet embrace those values may be aligned with their higher self so that they too might come to see themselves in others and embrace unity. This is the way of the Christ Consciousness.

21

CORPORATE WRONGDOING

*T*o undo separation and meet your system with the love of the Christ Consciousness, you must understand how the intersection of the criminal system and your corporate system are failing you because they are designed to keep a current structure of monetary flow intact. Yes, *intact*, because you would otherwise see an entirely different structure. And this is the way in which corporations are ultimately protected from a criminal justice system built on punishment and separation. Corporations escape the confines of a prison system that would otherwise confine them. That is what money has afforded them, for they are able to claim that the effect of imprisonment on a corporation would affect too many people.

Your system is therefore built on the idea that some entities must be protected because they are essential to the whole, even though they operate to the detriment of the whole. And yet this same logic does not apply to those individuals whom you separate and put in jail. You believe that somehow their separation is essential to your survival, and that their separation does not harm the whole, and this is in fact wrong. It is actually incredibly harmful to the collective that you separate and confine individuals for all manner of behavior. And yet you do not understand this, for you can only understand the ripple effects in a very limited manner.

Do you know what happens to a family when one member who has been convicted of what you have deemed to be a crime is then separated and sent to prison, and then cannot find a job afterwards? The ripple effects on their family and other families and communities are enormous. But you only evaluate the ripple effects based on your limited view of how it might affect you personally, rooted in your concern for self-preservation. You do not see those effects as extending beyond an individual. You do not look at the ripple effects over time or in the aggregate, and therefore you can only conclude that separation through punishment and confinement is the right course of action.

But when it comes to corporations, you do not do this. You do not look at them and say, *You are now confined. You can no longer conduct yourself in the same manner.* This is because you have generated an entity that is composed of many individuals and that is connected to many individuals in ways that you protect. And then the entity does something it shouldn't, but you do not blame the entity, you blame the constituent parts, you go ahead and separate them and say, *The entity is not to blame, no, it is an individual who did this.* Therefore you protect the entity, when in fact it is the entity that is to blame.

How is the entity to blame and not the individuals who acted?

Could the individual in question that you have now punished or fired been able to do what he or she did without the entity? No. So it is the entity who is still an integral part of what transpired, but your system separates them to protect the money-making potential of that entity. And so you do not say to the person who committed a crime, *We are only going to put away the part of you that caused this. We'll put away that small piece of you.* No, you put the entire body away. But not so with the entity—the corporation or company—at fault. And so you permit them to use their powers to accumulate and pool money, to simply expend a portion of it, and then continue. And we wish to draw your attention to the numerous ways in which this is extremely deleterious to your society, and how you might go about reforming it. It is deleterious because it fails to actually change the energy that needs to be changed.

Some people might say that this does not make sense. Didn't you say earlier that corporations do not have consciousness? If this is about regulating corporations, why are you speaking of changing their energy?

What is the difference? You understand that the power to regulate is simply the expression of energy in the form of words given authority because of your collective agreement. So there is little difference whether you regard this as regulation, as you currently do, or in terms of energy that alters the consciousness of the entity or corporation. For you understand that these are creations at the level of language, and they have a consciousness of their own, as all creations do. That is the nature of energy. It has a consciousness that isn't the same as yours or another person's. But entities have a consciousness, which is created out of the collective consciousness of those who make up and run the entity.

You cannot simply operate in the way you have without understanding that what needs to change is the consciousness of a corporation or company. The concept of a corporation as a legal entity that is both able to function like a person and able to function without the limitations of a person is not permissible. By allowing it, you have set up a structure that permits people to act in ways they would not if they were held responsible for their actions. They do so in the name of the corporation, and the consciousness of the corporation continues afterwards, having been able to conduct business in the name of the company without any form of accountability. The corporation does not take responsibility for its actions. No, it simply cuts away the pieces of itself that were found to be at fault and then continues on. It is this structure that you have created, which you have failed truly regulate or transform and is responsible for much of the social ills in your world.

So how do you change it? How do you go about altering this paradigm? Again, you must embrace a more accurate view of what it is you have created. You have created an entity that has all the benefits and powers of a person, without any accountability. What do we mean by that? The corporation no longer has to regard the free will of others. It remains immune from any of the karmic consequences of its mistreatment of others' free will. Consider the numerous incidences of corporate malfeasance that come to light again and again and again in your realm, and ask yourself, *What should be we do differently?* You come up with rules, rules that are rooted in language and interpretation, that the corporation then looks at and says, *We can do* this *instead*. And it will continue to look for those opportunities, for it is has one purpose: to accumulate money.

By enabling that basic purpose, and not holding it accountable in the way that people are held accountable, it can disregard the needs of people and the planet.

Your banks and corporations do this all the time. They steal from their customers, they pollute the earth, they do all manner of things because they ultimately are not held accountable. They will instead be able to use the very thing for which they were built—money—to simply escape their karmic obligations. You must begin to regard the corporation just as you would a person, and then you must begin to see that the accumulation of wealth is not something that can be permitted without accountability. And this might mean that corporations, the legal fictions that you have created, are ultimately dissolved quite easily; that you permit their dissolution and abandonment as a means of correcting their behavior. Can you see this as a possibility that you have forgone because you believe that the effects of dissolving them are too great? This is a lie that you tell yourselves.

Doesn't this mean we are replicating a paradigm of punishment that we need to surpass?

You think that this means you will punish everyone. You will begin to see the absurdity of the system you have created when you begin to treat corporations as people who may be jailed and prevented from doing business. For you will begin to appreciate the effects you have on others, and then you will begin to see them as different, but in ways that no longer privilege the accumulation of wealth and money over the accountability for their actions. This is fundamental to your survival. The corporation has allowed your society to privilege the accumulation of wealth over all other relationships and forms of creation. This has distorted your relationship to each other in fundamental ways.

So you must align to the possibility of a new way of organizing yourselves, of new structures that do not privilege and prioritize the accumulation of wealth, whose investment is not in growth, but instead can be measured by something else. And you can hold them accountable in ways that do not permit them to use that wealth as a means of escaping responsibility. This has played too great a role in the latter half of the past century and the first quarter of this current one; you have endured so many negative karmic effects as a result of this structure, of permitting a corporation to inflict pain on others without fear of consequence. Align to the possibility that there is another way of organizing, that the corporation can be dissolved, transmuted, gotten rid of as a structure that you permit and co-create with each other. Something new must come in its place.

22

COMING INTO UNITY

*W*e have explained that your system of taxation distributes money in ways that are dictated by those who have command of monetary resources that many do not have. And we have already spoken about the construct of the corporation, and how this structure allows for the accumulation of wealth and power in ways that are not available to so many of you. So you can see how the pieces of the machinery come together to create the system that ensures that money flows toward those who already have it.

What would another system look like? You already know the answer to that question insofar as it used to be the case that corporations could not exert nearly the influence they had on the political system because they were not afforded the same opportunity to spend their pools of money on elections. They did so with lobbyists, yes, with those who would speak on their behalf and speak directly to the politicians whose decisions could affect them. But a system existed—and could exist again—in which corporations are not allowed to contact and influence politicians through vast sums of money in the way that they do now. That much is obvious. And why you continue to labor under the assumption that no such system is possible makes no sense to us, as we watch your evolution. It makes no sense that you continue to create a system, and to rationalize it with words, from your Supreme Court, to support this inequitable and unjust system.

But how do you, at the level of consciousness, relate to this system? How do you relate to it and bring to it the frequency of the Christ Consciousness? For that is ultimately how you must relate to each and every system. You must relate to each and every system through the vehicle of the Christ Consciousness and thereby bring the energy of the Christ, the energy of unconditional love, to that entity or structure.

We will begin to explain how you align with the Christ Consciousness in a way that reverberates through these systems. It is not the usual way of doing business, so to speak. You cannot go into these systems and alter them through the very same mechanisms you have already created, have already used, for those systems are designed to ensure that these structures remain in place; that is their function. You foolhardily believe that someone new you elect every four to eight years can simply walk into a system that is entirely dysfunctional because it is built on separation and somehow achieve unity consciousness, as if everyone would all start working together in unison, with the same goals and aspirations.

No, this is folly, yet you believe the illusion whenever you elect a new President, as if this person's hands weren't already tied.

Nor is this going to happen simply because you believe that the courts got it wrong and complain and request that a new case be brought that changes the law. And while it is certainly laudable to see the law change, the law changes because the frequency of the collective consciousness has shifted, which then justifies the change in law.

So what do you do? You relate to that system with the same level of unconditional love and affection that you would bring to any other relationship where you are embodying the Christ Consciousness. This will seem utterly unfamiliar; it will seem entirely foreign to you. You will not understand what it is you are doing, because no one has ever related to the system in the same manner as we are describing. No one in the history of humankind has regarded their political system as a blessing to be loved unconditionally. Does this sound preposterous? Yes, but you will understand that by doing so you are directly injecting the frequency of the Christ Consciousness into that realm.

For so many of you, this is a blind spot. You regard politicians and your political system as beyond reform and full of crooks and swindlers who are only there to appease their own material needs. Yet you must relate to the system in the same way. You must accept it, and bring to it the type of energy that you would bring to any other relationship. You must meet it where it is and then align to a higher possibility, to a higher possibility than exists now, to the possibility of decision-making and choices that reflect a higher ideal, an ideal rooted in compassion and forgiveness and equality. That is what you do.

Do not get mired in the stories of those who write about the political system. Do not get caught up in the binary thinking of who is right and who is wrong, and which candidate is winning and which one is losing, and where is there corruption, and where is there power. All of those typical relationships with the political system must be jettisoned and ignored as simply one more manifestation of the collective consciousness.

Instead, you must regard it as a dance, as a play of light and dark, where you can see the gift of a political system in which there are efforts to protect rights and ensure certain benefits for the many. You can see that, in many cases, the system operates well enough to ensure that the system functions. The government operates, and people are able to do their jobs and travel and get places, and cities and states are running and operating. You can appreciate that this system is working to some degree, and that as a result, life continues to operate at the level of political structures. Your city governments work, your state governments work, all to provide necessary benefits and considerations.

So you can begin to appreciate that beneath all of it, beneath the darkness, there is light at work. The system is working but you can align it to a higher version of itself, to something more. It may take time to continually refine your sense of what is happening in the world and how you align to the possibility of a greater future than currently exists. But it can be done. It cannot be done by simply entering the system and playing the game. No, you must relate to the system through the eyes of the Christ Consciousness, and in so doing bring to it the Light of the Christ Consciousness.

❄

Despite the fact that so much of your system works, your current political system appears to be unraveling before your very eyes. Many of you wonder, *What can be done? What power do we have to alter this?* This system seems too powerful to undo, and therefore you opt to check out, to ignore it, to delve into all manner of other forms of entertainment and take your attention away. We understand your impulse to look away from your creation, or to judge it and say, *This is madness, this is insanity.* All versions of the same judgment, mind you. You do this and then wonder why the world is what it is. It is your responsibility, and we have said so. So how do you align to something else, to a different version of your political system? We have been showing you the ways that your system is corrupt and afflicted, and you wonder, *What can I do about it?*

The first way is to recognize that what you perceive is always a mirror of what is happening internally. Yes, it is always happening internally to some degree, and that makes it your responsibility to turn inward. It is not your responsibility alone to deal with the external manifestation of what occurs. But it is necessary for you to begin to deal with the internal state that you are currently holding. Yes, you hold an internal state, and this state is what you are resonating with externally. This shows you how so many of you are externally resonating with certain types of manifestations, of political systems that you don't want.

This is not a question of blame. This is a question of responsibility, which is to say that you are creators of your world. Now accept and embrace your creation. Do you wish to create something else? Then stop creating the same thing over and over again. You all search again and again for signs of inspiration, and you share lots of videos and snippets and stories of humanity doing good, and you say, this is beautiful, this restores my faith in humanity, look at how good it makes me feel. So why not do some of that good yourself? Why not go out and create something different?

This is the truth: You are not interested in the result; you are interested in how you *feel*. And so you look for what makes you feel a certain way. What you are escaping is the sense of a void, the sense of your own inner darkness, through a momentarily glimpse of Light. But this is light reflected off a lake or reflecting off the moon. It is a light reflected. It is not Light directly in your face, illuminating you. You need to be that Light. You need to go out and do the things that inspire and captivate others.

How does this work with your political system? Yes, this seems to be a difficult area for many of you, for even the brightest lights seem to dim the minute you hit the political world. Why? Because you forget all that you are and become absorbed in the terms of the game of politics. Notice that we did not say to become a politician. We did not say you should run for office or try to clean up politics. This is you trying to clean up a system through the very same means that others have. No, this is where you forget your power.

The first thing you must do is stop entering the political realm through the journalism and reporting that you currently produce, for it is all part of the same problem. Journalism and politicians are in a circular system, each producing the other, so that one does and says something you call "crazy" and then others "report" this, and then you read it and say, "crazy" and this creates a vicious circle. They are all part of a single maelstrom of linguistic creation.

This energy is very dense and very low; it is nothing more than judgment and hatred. That is really all your political discourse is: the paradigm of separation writ large. And so we ask you to no longer go into alignment with that discourse. Do not go into alignment with it by reading about it constantly.

Are we saying to ignore the news and go watch some TV or pretend that it is not there? No, we are not saying this. We are saying do not *align* with it. Do not engage with it through the same level of discourse. Do not criticize and call each other "stupid" or "crazy" or whatever terms you choose. Do not go into the feeling that it generates for you. These are stories you are generating, and they create energy. They contain energy. And you go into alignment with that energy and bring it into your own system.

You must separate yourself from that energy by not aligning to it, by relating it to it in a different manner. And that is to watch this language, recognize it for what it is, and begin to understand why each actor in this scenario, in this vivid tableau you call *politics*, is engaged in what they are doing. They are engaged in an act, a performance, for their own benefit, and they are driven by their egos, so begin to watch with some empathy for what they are doing, and begin to watch for the ways that you no longer empathize with those who seek only to protect themselves, but instead judge them. That is your first step in avoiding the alignment with the frequency of political discourse as it exists in your realm today.

23

WHAT IS TO COME

*T*he truth of the matter is that you do not know what
is to come. You cannot know, because if you knew,
you would inevitably chart a course to get there that
would lead you elsewhere. This is the way the mind works. For
in the process of trying to chart the course, you inevitably get
off course, for the mind will try to take you to places it thinks it
knows are the right ones for your destination, though they never are. We are telling you this because we cannot give you a blueprint for exactly where you need to go. No, we cannot give you
a template to fill out and just start building, for even if you had
it, you could not construct it with the minds you currently have.
You would not be able to do so with your present consciousness.

We ask that you instead alter the way you relate to the institutions and structures that currently exist. Think of them as
relationships, just like relationships with people, and much of
what we have taught you about bending space and time applies

equally to them. For they are energetic beings, just as your relationships with other people are. There really is no difference. They exist as the collective manifestation of your energy in relationship to an idea. That is, you all think of your government, and there is a collective energy from each and every one of you, as Seeds of Light, that generates what your government currently is.

And it is this relationship to the very idea of governing that must begin to change. For this is where you run into problems. Your efforts to make changes always involve reiterating the same structural problems and substituting new content. Yet it is the structure that must be undone, and you cannot do that by building with the consciousness as it currently exists in humanity.

The same applies to the structure of justice, to ways in which you judge and evaluate and punish people. The same applies to the relationship with the economic systems, the ways in which you allow the energy of money to flow and pool and collect and be redistributed. The same applies to the ways in which you relate to entire swaths of humanity through the nation-state, and through other structures such as your military, or your systems of communication like the Internet.

Yes, these are all energetic beings unto themselves. The only way to truly and fundamentally alter them is to alter your relationship to them. Because you are in a relationship of co-creation with them, they too will alter when you change your way of thinking. You cannot force the change, just as you cannot cajole or persuade someone into becoming a different person. Yes, they might change their external behavior, they might act differently, but until their internal state changes, this will be a superficial performance, a façade. Yes, you must go beyond the surface and construct a new society, one whose foundation rests on the Christ Consciousness. You must do this in relationship to your education system, to your media, to your government, to your military, to your banks, to your judiciary, to all of these systems that structure and organize how you relate as a collective.

This is the crux of our teaching and the central message of this book: how to relate as the Christ Consciousness to these larger systems and structures that now organize your world. Understand that this is no small task, for the pull of your collective consciousness is strong, particularly around these issues. The energy is great because there are so many other Seeds of Light invested in the status quo, in the structure as it exists. It is one thing to bend time and space in relationship to another person, and to work with the energy of the Christ in and through your relationship with that person.

Yet how do you bring the energy of the Christ Consciousness to the system of government? It is the same way as working with an individual. Even though you may be taking actions that look the same, as if you were acting from mass consciousness, your intention is what has changed.

For we are not suggesting you sit on a mountain and simply imagine a pretty new world, one that looks nice from the outside, some idyllic realm that you conjure up in your creative imagination and hope that the rest of the world picks up on. Many of you exit the realms that we are describing (i.e., politics, finance, etc.) because they do not conform to your views of what the world should look like, and you believe there is no place for you in them. So you ignore them. You walk away and say, *I will stay at an ashram or a monastery* or *I will live in this small, circumscribed realm, and I will not sully myself by entering into these other realms.*

This is an abdication of your responsibility. You *are* those other realms, which are part of the collective consciousness, because they are part of your awareness. You cannot escape. You cannot simply rush to a retreat center and pretend the rest of the world is not with you. You are still in it. You are simply ignoring it. We are teaching you how to relate to these areas of your world in a manner consistent with the Christ Consciousness, so that you can change those structures. That is what we have been doing all along in this book.

24

WHEN CHANGE HAPPENS

*W*e *have been speaking of* change and how you go about creating change by aligning to its possibility. We wish to speak now of how you relate to time as a measure of change in your present circumstances and how much you wish for the world to change *now*, and how you wonder when the world is going to improve. *When are we going to get there? When are going to heal entirely?* And we understand that this is difficult for you.

Time is the manner in which you relate to the horizon of change. Many of you want change to happen now, as if the present moment were not perfect already. Yes, we understand that you wish to experience a different reality, but you go about making change through all forms of persuasion and cajoling and pressuring and pushing, and none of this, we tell you, is going to result in the outcome you desire. No, it will not. You are resisting the present moment just as it is. So you must, as you do in all areas of where you propose to do spiritual work, embrace the present as it is. Embrace the political system, the economic system, the financial system, the judicial system, the educational system, the corporate structures that you have created—all of it. You must *accept* it.

That does not mean you *align* to it and hold it as the highest expression of what can be. No, that is not what we mean. We mean that you simply acknowledge that this is your reality and instead of rejecting it, condemning and blaming it, you acknowledge and accept it. You are, after all, in *agreement* with it. It is your creation and you are with it in this realm, so you are in agreement with it. It cannot be otherwise.[1]

But to be in *alignment* with it is another matter. You do not have to align with it as if it were the only way that life can be. No, you can begin to align to something higher without rejecting it, without looking at it and saying, *This is terrible, this is an abomination, this is a travesty.* That is what you do now, and you further entrench patterns of thought that are rooted in judgment and separation. This means that you simply accept the status quo as it is, as a perfect reflection of your collective consciousness in this moment. It is that simple. And then you *simultaneously* hold onto the possibility of something else, opening yourself to something else that can come, opening yourself to the idea that it can come and you will be available to receive it.

This means you align yourself to the possibility that there is some other way to be in this realm, in each of those domains, that allows for inclusion and unity, and does not privilege the ego and its machinations, such as greed and self-protection at the expense of others.

This is what you must do, but you can only align to another area if you have done the work that we have described in our previous books. Otherwise, you duplicate and replicate and re-produce yourselves in the same manner, with different forms of the same structure. They look new, but they are founded in the same patterns and same mental structures you began with.

So to align with these future possibilities, possibilities that exist at the level of energy but have not yet been made manifest, you must open yourself to the possibilities for inclusivity that you have not seen or experienced. They are not about judgment or retribution or condemnation or winning. That is your current model. Do not align yourself to the possibility that bankers and other people who have committed egregious wrongs are just sent to jail and then the world will be right. No, this will not accomplish the final emancipation you seek.

Are you saying that we should not send bankers who commit crimes to prison?

No, we are not saying that. This is your form of punishment. But you may continue to ask, as you do this, *Is this going to solve the problem?* Is this going to eliminate the issue that you see and instead construct a better system, one that is more inclusive? No, it is not. So you might feel the sense of satisfaction that bankers could no longer engage in the conduct they did that led to the harms inflicted on others. But they are just sitting in prisons, and someone else will do something else that will inflict harm, and so you have not really changed anything. There is no deep transformation.

Instead, ask yourself, *What kind of system based on inclusion and forgiveness could emerge? What types of options would be available instead if those were the guiding principles?*

You may be surprised at what you will see. At each moment, ask when you are in relationship to one of these systems, *How else could this system work?* We are not saying that you are necessarily going to change it all overnight. That is our point. The timeline for change is going to be very slow, for there are a great many Seeds of Light that form the collective consciousness, and the changes that occur are slight in comparison. But when you are in relationship to any one of these systems—and by *in relationship* we mean that you are engaged with them either in your own lives, or talking about them with others, or simply thinking about them, or reading about them in the news—do not fall back into your old habits of thought.

This is what the majority of you do; this is how you relate to them. You sit on a meditation cushion and you think lovely thoughts, and then you see a politician or a banker or someone involved in one of these systems, and you think, *That person is terrible. They're a crook. They're a horrible human being.* You think these thoughts, and you fall right back into the collective consciousness. That is what you do. And you must rise above this, and you must align with another possibility. That is what we mean when we say that you must relate to these differently, for your engagement with them is part of the co-creative process.

This is your power to align with a higher possibility, to align with the possibility of the Christ Consciousness as it bears on each of these realms.

25

LIBERTY AND NEW POSSIBILITIES

To bring the Christ Consciousness to bear on these realms is to *liberate* them from the collective consciousness. *Liberty* is a word that means a great deal to this country, and to the rest of the world. But liberty here is something you must begin to articulate in a new manner, in a different way, for it occupies a singular place in your history, in the history of your nation. To exercise liberty, to have freedom—the other word that you often use—means one thing to you, and something else to us.

We have a different concept of liberty and freedom, and that is what we want you to think about. Your society and your political and legal culture view liberty within specific terms, within specific identities, and your country believes that certain people are free and others are not. One of the many constrains on your concept of freedom is that you often see freedom only in relationship to oppression and limitation.

This is not accurate. We understand that certain groups of people are treated as less or do not receive society's full benefits, but that does not mean that they are not free, that they do not exercise any liberty. So our first point is that you must begin to *uncouple* liberty and freedom from the notions of constraint or discrimination that currently occupy much of your understanding of what it means to be human. You diminish everyone's power to exercise freedom and liberty when you only see freedom in the absence of discrimination.

The other aspect of your concept of liberty and freedom, and this appears deeply in your legal culture, is that there are certain items or tasks or activities, ways of being, that are considered very fundamental to what it means to be human, and must be protected, and we applaud this. These are things like the right to choose who you get to claim a relationship of life and love with, or the right to life or the right to procreate, and these various freedoms are certainly essential to what it means to be free and human. But this is not the only way to conceptualize liberty.

This is where we must begin to *broaden* your concept of liberty, broaden it much beyond what you see because you are already limiting the concept of liberty by ensuring that it replicates the past, that it replicates the known identities and the known activities of your past.[1] We are not saying don't protect them, that they are not to be cherished and allowed to flourish. No, that is not our point. Our point is that there is much more to liberty, and that the liberty of which we speak is one that does not have any constraints imposed by the past.

Well, how does that work for the law?

The answer is not yet clear, not because we are avoiding it, but because you must make your way there. But it is certainly

possible that there are ways of conceptualizing liberty and freedom that would not in any way be limited those that your
Constitution has decided are protected. The Supreme Court
of your country has interpreted that word to mean one thing,
and that determines when that collective agreement, that bind-
ing document, affords a certain amount of protection. But that
does not mean your concepts of liberty need to be so limited.
No, we believe that you ought to consider that liberty is nothing more than the right to infinite possibilities and infinite creation that does not in any way preclude another Seed of Light
from exercising their free will to co-create their own reality.

Do you understand how basic and yet radical this notion
of liberty is? Do you not see that this would mean that any instance where you decide to create and exercise your creative capacities, to become whatever it is you seek to become, that does
not inhibit the ability of other Seeds of Light to exercise their
same authority, is freedom? Do you not see how simple and yet
wide-reaching this is?

*Is that even possible? Wouldn't there be instances where you
would be inhibited?*

Yes, and we are not here to elaborate on all the possible
permutations of where one person's creation will run into another person's creation and their free wills might conflict, and
therefore they must respect each other's autonomy as Seeds of
Light with free will, which means that they will alter and shape
their creations accordingly. But would you even describe someone's creations that denied another's free will as an exercise of
liberty? No, you would not. The Christ Consciousness would
not seek to create in a way that denied another their capacity
to create.

But do you not understand what it would mean to allow any and all forms of liberty? People would do many, many things that are not permitted now; not by law, we are not speaking of law, but of social convention. Again, do you realize how much of your lives are spent in limitation due to social conventions?

That is the point of liberty, and that is the point of being in a human body with limitless potential for creation. This means that at each instance, you can ask yourself, *What more is possible? What haven't I tried? What else can be done here that hasn't been done before or that I simply haven't tried or done before?* And when you open to that infinite possibility, the world opens up in so many other ways. That is the notion of liberty that we want to see instilled in your society. That is the notion of liberty that is fundamental to the Christ Consciousness. That notion encompasses those types of liberties you already seek to protect and promote as part of your Constitution, but it is so much more. It is up to you to begin to explore your freedom in all areas of society and ask, *How else could this be done?*

26

RELATING DIFFERENTLY
TO THE WORLD

*W**e have spoken of your* tendency to fall into old patterns when it comes to how you engage with the political and social realms, and we have spoken of how you must align yourself to other possibilities, to infinite possibilities, but this is not done without some effort.[1] We understand that this requires the effort to continually release your judgment and look at the world with different eyes, with divine eyes. By this we mean that you must look upon the world as being in perfect, divine order now, not as something that is flawed, with a future moment bringing something better or even perfection. No, look at it *now* as the instantaneous creation of divine perfect order, as a measure of your current state of consciousness.

You are moving toward perfection, and by that we mean you are moving toward releasing the structure of the ego as created by the collective consciousness, rooted in judgment, separation, and exclusivity, and you are moving toward unity. And this is what we mean by the Christ Consciousness: unity in all beings as you realize that your differences are mere play, they are the multiplicity of all forms of life. The opportunities that are available to you to express yourself differently in form are incredible. They are a joy, they are a gift, but instead you rally around those differences as if they were something to be protected and defended, and they are not.

You all fall into old patterns when you encounter these areas of your world; it is not an easy thing to avoid. We understand the difficulty of embracing the Christ Consciousness in these areas. It is far too easy to think, *I will be spiritual here, in this area, in my private life, with a few select people and not with the rest of the world. Over here, in this other area, I will rail and rant and judge and yell because I need to be heard, we all need to be heard.* But this is not true. This is not true at all. This is where you must align and release expectations. That is the primary downfall for all of you: You have expectations of how it should look and on what timeline, and this means you get impatient, you get fed up when the world doesn't shift dramatically and conform to your views of how it should look and how people should behave.

This is just another manifestation of the collective consciousness at work. You have fallen into judgment; you have fallen into separation. It is not easy to regard with unity all of your brothers and sisters, your fellow Seeds of Light, who act in the most misguided ways, who embrace and identify with the collective consciousness, and who defend the systems that permit them to protect themselves at the cost and expense of others. Do not forget that you do these things too in your own way, even as you regard yourself as further along the path, and even though you may be shining brighter. It is here that your light dims again as you return to your old ways.

So the key is to again align to a greater possibility, to ask what other possibilities are there. With any upcoming election, align to the possibility that the right outcome is in fact occurring, that what you will experience is precisely what needs to occur for you all to grow into unity. That's what you can do, and you can hold the possibility, hold and align to the possibility, which means that you stand for it, and feel it as if it were true already in your body, in your world, that they will choose a path based on love and unity and not on fear. That you can do at each instance.

By holding, *what do you mean? Can you elaborate on this alignment process?*

You align by holding it in your creative faculties and in your body as the reality that you are experiencing. You embrace it not with hope, not the with the idea that "this is good if it happens, but it might not," not with any sort of gap between you and the outcome, but by holding the energetic feeling in your body, by feeling it in your body now, as if that were reality, because it is your reality, at a quantum level. And so you align by dispensing with the creation of negative energies you know so well, and by instead aligning with and attuning to the frequencies of the energies that you know are the ones that will elevate.

So imagine, if you will, the outcome an election in which you hope that unity and peace will prevail over disunity and greed and anger and hatred. And imagine that you know many people who are scared or angry or upset and want nothing more than to attack and tear down a system that they feel has betrayed them. Can you still hold them in your heart, along with the possibility of change? Can you hold them in your heart and mind's eye, and imagine that they will choose a path of love?

Do not judge them and write them off and say they are crazy. That is your way now, and that is the path of the collective consciousness. That is the very path that has them choosing hatred and fear over love. So hold them in your mind's eye as doing what is best for the collective good, for their good, for the good of all humanity, and see what transpires. This means accepting what happens, however it happens, and still aligning to the possibility that this is the best outcome for ultimate growth. That is what you must do. That means you must be very vigilant with your thoughts and feelings, and continually return yourself to the frequency of the Christ Consciousness. You must co-create yourselves with them, stand in the space of co-creation with other Seeds of Light, with the firm belief and conviction that you are co-creating a better reality.

❈

We wish to give you a tool to relate to the rest of the world differently. You must begin to relate to the rest of the world as you did with your relationships with others, by bending time and space. And this what we have meant by allowing the other to co-create as they choose, and for you to be able to meet them where they are and still co-create with the possibility that the other will relinquish their past and co-create something different.

Now this seems very straightforward when you are dealing with a marriage or a parent or some sort of relationship where there are two of you. But how do you move beyond that and work with entire communities? Yes, there are still actions to be taken and you must learn to engage and speak, but it is *how* you must speak and engage that we wish to address. We will then provide you a tool, a verbal formulation, that you can use as you continue to align with a greater possibility.

You must engage with the larger community as a relationship; you have a relationship with that community. It has an energy, and that energy has consciousness. For some of you that relationship is anger or apathy or something like that. It is almost always filled with judgment.

That is the *sine qua non* of separation, and so there is judgment. You regard those who are part of whatever community you are designating—and by "community" we mean any collection of individuals united around a purpose, whether it be politicians or judges or bankers or economists or police. Those are united in their common purpose, and therefore you have a relationship to them, and this appears in your thoughts and judgments of them when you say that "politicians are ____" and you fill in the blank with some sort of judgment or evaluation or insult. This is what you do, and therefore you write them off and co-create them as such with others who share the same view of this type of relationship, and that relationship, as we have said, has its own energy, its own consciousness.

So you must begin to relate to them differently, despite the behavior and actions of those who appear to be beholden to their own self-interests and act in ways consistent with the collective consciousness. Yes, we want you to begin to relate to them as relationships that deserve the same type of love and the same type of compassion as when you are dealing with a single Seed of Light. Yes, you are bringing compassion. You will meet them where they are, without judgment, and still align to the possibility of a higher consciousness that is available to them now. By doing so you help co-create them differently. You can begin to do this by your own internal thoughts, and by sharing your own internal thoughts rooted in compassion and non-judgment with others. You thereby give voice to that energy, spreading the energy of compassion through them and nullifying the energy of judgment that currently dominates your discourse.

Now, this is not easy. You will always find another instance, another example, of someone who seems to justify their exclusion and separation from the rest of you because of their behavior. This you must resist, for you are entrenching further the very structures of thought that have given rise to the problem. We know that we repeat, but we must repeat, for you immediately find someone to draw you out of that state of acceptance and back into the past patterns from which you have been trying to elevate yourself. You immediately co-create yourself in the now, in the moment, with the past grievance and judgment you have attempted to relinquish. You have given the grievance and judgment life again. You have resurrected them—this is your power.

You must approach this relationship differently, and this is the verbal formula we wish to give you so that you can remind yourself. It is similar to the one we gave you before, but we want you to use the names of the individuals or their category or their entire system.

Political system, judicial system, etc. or politicians, bankers, etc.,
I stand before you and accept you just as you and forgive you for

the creation you have made. By forgiving you, I meet you where you are now, and align with the possibility that we will co-create a future rooted in compassion and love, not separation. I am the Christ, and I am the Christ through you. You are the Christ, and you are the Christ through me. Amen.

This kind of formulation is important because we must extend this energy to other realms, to other dimensions of your planet, and we must do so now, quickly, as the increasing tempo of the changes in your system requires and demands more and more alignment with the higher frequencies that are emerging. For this is what is happening now on your planet.

As you see more and more turmoil, understand that what is happening has been boiling beneath the surface and is now coming up for release, coming up to be released and forgiven and not reborn, as you co-create and resurrect yourselves anew. We need to extend the energy of the Christ Consciousness, the energy of forgiveness and compassion and unity to all of these realms. You cannot limit it to just one realm, to the world of the yoga mat, the meditation cushion, or to your personal finances. No, you must bring this energy to all facets of your world, to society at large, in all of the areas where you feel the most judgment and where you have created the most separation because of the influence of money and the corporate structure. Realize that this is your mission, all of you reading this: to transcend the ego in all areas of your life, not just your interpersonal world or a smaller community of seekers. No, you must begin to spread the word of the Christ Consciousness to other realms. Now, now, now.

✳

All of these realms that you must relate to through the lens of the Christ Consciousness can be understood together through the word *demos*. An important concept in your realm, demos is the idea that each of you has a voice in the collective functioning of your society through someone who represents you. What you are moving toward is a different concept of the demos, a different way of approaching the collective whole, rather than through judgment and trying to win, aligned with political parties, and using vast resources to convince everyone that the other person is wrong. You split along binary axes in ways that make no sense, and solely to distinguish yourselves so one side can claim victory over the other, and one side can claim this position of power over another.

None of it is real. So much of what you do has nothing to do with reality as it is. You reduce reality to very superficial frameworks that people can grasp and put a position in one box or another—Republican or Democrat, liberal or conservative. These are your boxes, as if they were the only ones. Your task is to ask, *Where can I participate in this realm, where can I have a voice that is not aligned with these binaries, but is aligned with the collective as a whole?* Can you regard the collective binaries and not fall into judgment that either one is wrong? We are repeating ourselves once again for your benefit, yes, for your benefit.

To relate to each of these areas requires that you embody the Christ Consciousness with all of the Seeds of Light who embody and encompass that area. Do you realize that you now simply isolate individuals and blame them or write off the entire field, but never modify your relationship with or perspective on that domain or industry? No, you do not, and that is the fundamental task for all of you now. You are not going to individually pass new laws or remove certain individuals from higher offices or somehow fundamentally alter the structure as it currently exists. No, you are going to align with a different possibility, and you are going to give voice to the possibility that these areas are governed by compassion and unity, not greed and disunity. You are going to speak, and then others will move upward into the structures that exist and begin to articulate a different voice.

Imagine, if you will, that the world was not built on separation, and that there was a sense that everyone was capable of abundance, and that the amount that you needed was always available and sufficient. You would not be driven by greed, you would not need to make more than someone else to justify your self-worth, you would not try to accumulate vast quantities of money or material possessions to hold back the feelings of dissatisfaction. Your entire relationship to the enterprise of money would be different. And so you might find your financial institutions operating very differently, because the people who made them up were not invested in making money to feel better about themselves.

Instead, imagine if they saw their role as a divine one, of shepherding resources to other Seeds of Light, if they saw themselves in an infinite chain of love, where their work and efforts were enabling others to experience the fullness of their being, not, *What's in it for me?* Can you imagine what that structure would look like? No, but that is the basic premise of what the Christ Consciousness would bring to that structure. And so we will elaborate for you in other areas what some of the basic and fundamental characteristics of the Christ Consciousness would look like and how people might think of these areas.

27

A NEW MODEL OF JUSTICE

We have already said that much of your judicial system is built on punishment and winning and losing, determining who is responsible to make amends to another. Some of your judicial system is about punishment in the form of imprisonment, and some of it is about punishment in the form of money. Your system is built on what a judge thinks is the right outcome, and you have a very crude approach to how people act and behave that does not account for the complexity of the ego or the constructed nature of the collective consciousness. No, you base it on other things, things that you believe make an outcome seem just.

This is a very limited approach, for it is always the product of a judge's limited understanding of what transpired between the parties and who they are and not based on the karmic reasons for their conflict. Those karmic reasons are almost certainly beyond the purview of a judge, and so the punishment or decision never fully grasps the complexity of the relationship.

Typically what is at stake for you is a judge's ability to make a decision based on the parameters set out by the judicial system. In other words, you express concerns for bias and how the judge might act toward certain people and not others based on factors that should not be a part of the legal calculus the judge is meant to perform. You look at your system now and see enormous disparities. Those disparities are real. Many disparities have inflicted burdens on those of different races. Others are allowed to get away because of the type of act they committed, which makes it very difficult to pursue. It may be that some individuals are shielded as result of the fact that they work for a corporation, and there is no way for your system to determine that they are responsible in a way that a judge can make a meaningful decision.

You can argue for reforms, and you can hope that the law changes, but the ultimate concern is whether your judicial system can operate with a sense of divine justice, compassion, and morality. Those are the issues that you must address. And so we ask: What it would be mean if a judge were to take a different approach, and the lawyers who appeared in the judge's court room were all guided instead by the Christ Consciousness? What would that look like? It might mean that the considerations of the lawyers in pursuing a case or defending a case would be different, and would be able to accommodate the possibility that one or the other parties was in fact being driven by a different agenda or that they were not operating for the highest good, for divine justice, but for their own material greed. Perhaps that would lead other lawyers to counsel them differently, and not because they are being paid to defend or represent them, which leads many lawyers to take actions that are not based on a real assessment of what is going on but on a zealous advocacy or defense of their client, regardless of whether they actually believe it.

Perhaps judges would begin to shape their views of what the law says and think about it in ways that take a fuller picture of a human being, or see their role in a much broader sense. What if the judge were able to look at the litigants and not see two individuals, each with something to gain or lose, but a sense of divine justice and divine order? What if the judge could see them as byproducts of a collective consciousness, and accommodate the possibility of an outcome more nuanced than what is currently allowed, in which there are winners and losers? What if the judge began to see his or her role in a far greater sense of not simply adjudicating the matter before him or her but as a means of speaking more broadly to the collective consciousness and to the disparities in your system, and their ability to address them?

What if those were the types of judges and lawyers running your system? What would happen to the world of the law as you currently know it? How might lawmakers working in various states and at the federal level begin to act if they were driven by unity consciousness and the Christ, and not by the figure of separation and the need to control others?

You can align to the possibility of a different type of justice, a different approach to how justice and judges might mete out their decisions, so that punishment does not take the forms you have commonly understood them to be, and that justice is not always about inflicting some sort of separation or imposing a monetary penalty. The judges in your system might contemplate other forms of work, such as reconciliation and forgiveness, as a means of resolving disputes.

We ask you now to consider the connection between judges and your political system. Judges are protected in your system for the most part because they are often appointed for life. Many of them also hold very strong views about the nature of what it means to be human and how and why human behavior occurs, and there is nothing to correct this view. By virtue of having the position for life, judges remain immune from any challenges to their views, except through the standard processes that your system affords in its so-called "appeals" to a higher authority, to the next court up. Many judges act in ways that are consistent with their own views, and therefore come to conclusions based on how they think parties should behave and act. The result is that many judges are in a position to reinforce their normative views of the world, and therefore to extend the collective consciousness in the results that they choose for their decision-making. By occupying such an important role in the level of power in your society, judges who are absorbed by the collective consciousness are often not capable of understanding what it means to try something different, to resist the temptation to confine everyone or to impose penalties.

The temptation of judges to impose their views on those who come before them is great. This means that you will continue to have a system that metes out punishment in ways that do not conform to the Christ Consciousness, but instead reflects the standard views of the collective consciousness. Your judges are absorbed by that consciousness as well, and there is no reason to believe they are any more awake than others. For those who are in positions of power for life are given the freedom to indulge their own idiosyncrasies and views. Nothing requires them to challenge their views, and their views are shaped by the judicial practice that they see every day. They only come to see human beings in the ways that they are presented by the law, through the law's framework, and this can be deeply impoverishing.

So you must align with and consider as a part of your responsibility the task of broadening the ways that judges look upon humans. Do judges ever visit prisons? Do they ever visit the neighborhood or the settings where crime and punishment occur? Are they fully aware of the effects of their actions? Judges in your system are rarely confronted with the effects of their choices to wield the enormous power that society gives them, so they are often not aware of the impact of their actions. This is a distinct role for a select few in your society, and it is important for you to align to the possibility that they might have the opportunity to experience what they do when they send someone to jail or deport someone or engage in any decision-making that shapes the lives of the individuals before them. This is one way in which you can begin to call for a certain type of reform, to broaden the experiences of those judges who have never before stepped outside the confines of their court rooms. That possibility would also alter how justice, what your society calls justice, is meted out.

28

HOW TO VALUE PEOPLE

A ll of these questions about your judicial system share the same fundamental question: What do you value in another person? Yes, that question is important for seeing how you relate to all the systems in place. And the question has many meanings, it has many layers, for the first part is what do you value, by which we mean what aspects of the other person do you attach any significance or meaning to. As a second part, what aspect of that system or person do you not regard, and, third, how do you measure that value? Are you ranking certain aspects hierarchically or are you saying that those aspects are essential, necessary to the person's role?

We ask you to contemplate what it means to value something in another person. You assign different values to those who occupy public roles in politics, in the judicial system, and in the economic realm. You evaluate a candidate for office for their courage or their authenticity, and you evaluate those who build phones and laptops for the innovation and their creativity and their commitment to advancement and change. You do not necessarily value the same things in the same people. You evaluate them based on certain criteria that you believe are essential to the role that they are performing in the world.

Do you have a basis for those criteria? Do you know why you are so obsessed with authenticity and transparency and trustworthiness in your Presidential campaign, but not those same areas for the CEO of Apple? You may have criteria for bank officials but different ones altogether for other members of your society. Consider that the very criteria you use is often a based on misperception. Your valuation is in essence a form of judgment that has little bearing on who they really are and the role they play, and this leads to all forms of distortion in how you relate to these domains. You expect that your politicians be authentic, and you expect that your movie stars be down to earth, and you expect that your CEOs be another way.

Part you is saying, *Well isn't that logical, don't we want certain types of people in certain roles and certain types of people in others roles?* We do not say that seeking certain qualities is somehow wrong. No, we are not saying that. We are saying that *the qualities you do seek do not align with the role that you wish for them to fulfill.* That is the difference. We are suggesting that when you are engaging with these realms, you are seeking qualities that have something to do with you, and not with the task or role at hand. This creates a whole distortion of that entire field, of the way you relate to those in whom you seek certain qualities.

We began by talking about a politician and how you want this politician to be trustworthy, and you believe that this is the case when you believe they are authentic, so you believe you know them. This is very common, when in fact what you really want is not to "know" them; you want to know that they will perform the job that they were given, which is represent your interests and do what they said they would do.

Do you actually seek out the qualities that suggest that they do what they say, or do you seek out the qualities that make you feel good around them, make you feel that you know them? This is the difference of which we speak, that the way you align to these categories of individuals is often through a lens having to do with someone else. You seek the qualities that are actually relevant to a different role, a different role for someone to play in your life. And so you do not choose the "right" person for the role. No, you choose someone based on criteria that is actually for a different role, some other emotional role in your life. You do this with all manner of relationships, including friends and loved ones, but this is equally true of your relationship to those in your career, in the areas we have been describing of your society, of law, the economy, politicians, education, etc.

Why is this important?

It is important for how you align to and relate to these aspects of your society. For you are in judgment of them, you criticize them, when you see them perform in ways that are not consistent with your interests, and do not reflect the interests of society as a whole. They act in ways that are greedy and financially motivated or for power. And then you complain, you all complain about how terrible these people are, and politicians are all the same, and the Wall Street people just want to bilk us for our dough. Yes, you say all manner of judgmental statements.

Yet you have received exactly what you claimed when you sought out institutions and chose people based on criteria that would not lead them to protect your interests. You chose them for other reasons. Were those other reasons served? Perhaps. But are they the criteria designed to serve the issues you now say are not addressed? Did the candidate not do what he or she said but what some corporation said? Why does that surprise you when the corporation gave so much more money, and your system is built on influence through money? Why did the candidate do something that is consistent with their past actions? Because that is what they know how to do, and they acted consistently with their true views. They may have told you something else to procure a vote, but that is what your system is designed to do. It is designed to allow people to choose someone who can say that they are for this and then change their mind. That's the system you've designed.

Can you see the difference it would make if your system were not built the way it is—that is, if people didn't say they'd do one thing and then change their minds the minute you say yes and give away your vote? You could have a different system, one in which the person was evaluated by the public much more often, or where decisions made by the politician that were inconsistent with what they said that they would do would automatically mean they were removed from office. You see that this is a possibility, no? That could be the system. Now, some of you would say that system wouldn't work. Does your system work now? Does the system you currently have achieve the results you want of having individuals represent your views entirely and consistently?

If not, then the answer is that your system doesn't work either.

What we are trying to impress upon you now is how much you have all acquiesced in the face of systems that do not reflect the criteria that they are meant to serve. Instead, you value the people in them for other reasons, reasons having nothing to do with those systems. Then you complain that the system doesn't work, but you also don't change the system, you don't choose based on criteria that would actually be consistent with the purpose of the system, nor do you try to alter the system to ensure those criteria are met.

Your infinite capacity to create seems to be very limited when it comes to larger systems because you do not imagine, you do not think, about the different ways that the system could work. You fall prey to magnitude of the system, and say, *Who am I? Just one person.* No, you are a Seed of Light co-creating this entire realm with all the other Seeds of Light, and that infinite capacity to create is what allows you to align, to align with other possibilities, to claim them, with your intentions, thoughts, and words, and then your actions.

And this is what you must do. Your effect, each person's effect, may seem limited when dealing with the magnitude of systems like these, but that is only the perception of your mind. You must begin to align and call into being those systems that would reflect your unity, that would embrace inclusivity and reject exclusivity. You can do this in the ways that we have described, and we will continue to elaborate on in the remainder of this book.

❋

We are exploring the ways in which you all co-create with each other and produce in this very instant, at this moment, an institution or entity or structure as part of your society that grapples with the inherent separation that you have agreed to upon incarnating in this realm. Many of you struggle with moving beyond the relationship to yourself—to yourself, your past, and your ego—to the relationships with others like your parents or siblings or spouse or coworkers, neighbors. And further still to the relationships you have with social structures like the systems we have been discussing, which are made up with an enormous number of Seeds of Light. At each stage you are asked to relate to the relationship differently. Or at least that is what you think. You think that it is different when you deal with the larger structure than when you deal with yourself or your mother or your partner. But this is not true. It is the same— the scale is what leads you to confusion, but the relationship is the same.

You all grapple with race, sex, sexuality, etc. The same is true of the financial system, the political system, the law, and the education system. And while you do not identify with them in the same way, this does not mean you can withdraw from or escape them. Where would your money go? Where would you get an education? Where would you handle any legal issues that arose? You might say that you don't have any, but the truth is that you are all equally enmeshed in the same structures just as you are embodying gender, sexuality, race, etc. You might not be relating in the same way, but you cannot escape them. They are part of the collective consciousness.

It is how you relate to separation that dictates your mindset, the consciousness that you have. You can operate in terms of fear and greed and separation, or in terms of love and unity and compassion and forgiveness. You can bend time and space around you so that aspects of your life align with the frequency of the Christ Consciousness, and you can stand for the possibility of seeing another in their fullness.

All of this was an effort to get you to see each other, see other Seeds of Light for their divinity, in their fullness. Now, what kinds of relationships can you form from that? This was the topic of our last book. What kinds of social structures can you build from those relationships? That is the topic of *this* book. So you see, the relationship is the same. At all times, you co-create out of unity or exclusion, from the Christ Consciousness or the collective consciousness.

Isn't that just another binary?

It appears to be so, as we have framed it, because that is the way you can best position yourself to make a choice. But understand that this is actually a fiction insofar as there is always a clear answer. It is only because we are drawing you toward a singular possibility that we have framed it this way.

But for now, understand that the issue is that you are building a new society, not by enacting the same types of structures and entities that you previously formed, but by building out from the relationships you have with others founded on forgiveness, compassion, and unity.

So imagine, for example, a system of retribution or punishment that was infused with the frequency of the Christ Consciousness. How would the judges and police officers and prison guards operate? Would you have prison guards at all? Ask yourselves these questions. What if instead of punishment, there was some sort of community response to a crime? What if instead of separation, the individual who committed the supposed harm was instead required to connect more deeply with the community in ways that you would never consider? What if they were actually required to spend a month with each of the families in the community where they were harmed? Or what if you simply stood with the question: What is in the highest good for this individual who has acted misguided ways, who has acted out of separation?

Say this person took food or money or did something, driven by the ego and its belief in its separation from the rest of the world. Do you punish through the same means that you have used for thousands of years and which obviously have in no way altered humanity's consciousness for the better? No, you must ask: What forms of reconciliation and accountability and forgiveness and compassion are available to you that you simply do not use? Do you understand this is the awesome power that you wield? Your ability to choose other means of relating to each other in each of these settings is glorious and splendid.

As you watch the news (another area of your world that needs to be aligned with a much higher frequency of energy), ask yourself: How do you connect with each and every news story? Do you side with one party or the other? Do you side with the victim and judge and condemn the person who committed a crime? Do you wish this person harm and say good riddance? Do you say to yourself, *Oh, the world is really a mess, there is so much bad happening, in fact, it's getting worse?* As you do, you are co-creating the same negative storyline, again and again. Instead, you can ask yourself, *What other possibilities exist?* You see all sorts of evidence of this when you hear news stories of victims who instead of pursuing the harshest punishment chose instead to forgive their wrongdoers. You see them and they spread like little messages of hope, and you enjoy their courage and the good feelings they promote, and then you go about your business of putting people in jail.

This is folly, this is madness, and we ask you all to ask for something better. You can act on this. You can ask people to spread these messages, you can speak with those whom you've elected and ask, "Why is this not possible?" Ask yourself at all times, *Why is something else not possible?* Say to yourself, *I wonder what it would be like if . . .* and begin to articulate a different message, a different system. What if the people on Wall Street were not invested in their own wealth, but invested in the building of wealth for many? What if judges and police officers were not invested in the idea of safety and protection, and driven by fear and the need to punish and set the scales of justice right, but instead saw their task differently? What if they saw themselves as healers who were responsible for shepherding those who were ready to do harm because of their enormous pain, and responsible for helping them repent and take responsibility for their actions and seek forgiveness and chart a better course in life? How would this alter how they met all of the people who came within their purview? These and many more questions like it are the ones you must begin to ask. Your world depends on it.

29

SEEING UNITY IN THE WORLD

*W*e are deepening your understanding of how you must relate to society as a whole, and how the Christ Consciousness relates to society as a whole. For you have moved beyond the self and your own relationship to the self, and beyond your relationship to others around you, and you are now looking at the consciousness that encompasses all of it and relates to all of it without judgment, with compassion and in unity with all of it.

Can you look at the entire world around you and see unity, see the perfection in each instant? It might seem overwhelming, for you very quickly hone in on the negative aspects, what you perceive be to negative: crime, pain, suffering, poverty, and hunger. And we applaud your efforts to keep these in mind, but they are often too much of a distraction, for you do not also see the beauty, the harmony, the movement between order and chaos, that we do. We see the dance of life, as energy ebbs and flows, and manifests and takes form and then changes, and we see this constant movement between life erupting and death emerging, between light and shadow, and it is breathtaking in its spectacular beauty.

It is a vision to behold, and we ask you to begin to relate to that same vision in the same way, with joy and wonder and awe. We taught you to look at a person and see them with awe and wonder and ask, *What else might they show me today? What new facet have I not seen?*[1] Can you do the same with the world around you? Can you ask what else there is to be seen, and then look and see what is around you? Do you see people pushing and shoving each other to get some place, or honking their horns, or angrily waiting in a checkout line somewhere, staring at their phones, or do you see the ebb and flow of people who are being served, receiving the gifts of the labor of those who are giving them food or selling them a product, and to see them all working together, flowing through streets or in line, in agreement with each other as to the basic rules of the road so that they are operating in harmony?

Do you look at the world and see how much fusion and connection there is among people as they eat, sleep, drink, communicate, etc.? This is the dance of life as you each co-create each other in the moment, and there is so much beauty to behold. We know that you do not see it this way. Your headlines, news stories, and posts emphasize drama, scandal, and outrage. These are the baser emotions that provoke you, and you retort in kind with judgment and anger and outrage. And this is what you see: chaos and disaster.

But this is not the only way to view this. That view tells you about your consciousness, your perception, not the energy that is actually being emitted and formed at every moment. You simply need to expand your perspective and see this from a higher vantage point. See the movement back and forth, the interaction, as people move like cells through a body, all inter-connecting and weaving and exchanging energy so that there is a healthy whole. Look at the whole of your society and see how much beauty there is.

And from that perspective, you can begin to ask, *How can we bring more beauty? How can we create more unity? What it would it look like if in this community, there was more of what is available here in this other community?* And then you can begin to see what it would be like to create in those areas from the perspective of wonder and joy and contentment, not from the place of anger and outrage that you currently inhabit. So even though many of your areas may seem challenging, and there is a great deal of healing to occur in your world, embark on that task with a sense of adventure and wonder, of what possibilities can be created, not from a place of anger and judgment and reproach for what came before.

❋

We are speaking about how you are in relationship to these larger systems, just as you are in relationships with yourself and others. Resilience is the capacity to be with something where it is, what-ever it is, in the present moment; to be with that which you re-sist, and to maintain that relationship. And this is true of your relationship to the larger world, which you judge and condemn when it doesn't look like you think it should. When that happens, instead of maintaining resilience, you retreat. This is something so many of you do: You retreat from the world and profess that you are done with it, all in the name of personal growth and ascension, or move on because the world doesn't understand who you are. You've moved beyond it in some way; you're elevated.

This is not true. You are repressing your relationship to the world, trying to sever it, as if you were not in agreement with it. You are in agreement with it because you experience it as part of your consciousness. It is in your awareness, and so it is part of you. It cannot be otherwise. For if you had truly ascended, if you were truly in another vibrational dimension, then you would not be experiencing this realm. But the truth is that you are experiencing it because you agreed to experience it. Again, we do not say you are in alignment with it. That much is not true. You refuse to align by retreating.

But there is another way, and it requires the type of resilience that you have found hard to cultivate. You have found it hard to cultivate because it requires you to remain in contact with that which you don't like, with those who lead lives that seem to depend entirely on older paradigms of thought or are entirely aligned with the collective consciousness. You think that your contact with them corrupts and lowers you, that it burdens you. But it does not when you are truly present. When you are actually in your space as a Seed of Light, when you are aware of your fullness, the truth of your divinity, there can be no corruption. But that is not where most of you are at, and so what you are rejecting is not the collective consciousness, not the people that you believe you have ascended above. No, you are rejecting the part of you that falls into agreement with and even into alignment with the collective consciousness. You are rejecting that portion of you that is just like those other people.

That is not easy for many of you to hear. You wish to believe that you have transcended, but this is not always the case. You are still learning, and you may have aspects of yourself that are triggered by those who are in your world, in the world of the collective consciousness that you so desperately want to escape.

We understand this. But trying to artificially sever your ties is really just you cutting off bits and pieces of yourself without really loving them. It will not supply you with the emancipation you seek. You must instead cultivate resilience—to have something be a part of your life stream without falling into alignment with it, and yet not reject it and cut it out of your life stream, either. Can you hold this dual perspective? Can you be in the midst of the fights and the war and the drama and all that transpires daily and is reported by your media, and yet not fall into its trap? Can you be a part of the collective consciousness, bear witness to it, and at the same time not fall into identification with it? This is another word for alignment, but we have not used it because of the way in which identity is a reflection of your tendency to try to isolate and lay claim to your existence through certain categories of form. We prefer *alignment* rather than *identification*.

And so we conclude by saying that resilience is your capacity to remain with the collective consciousness, with these realms as they currently appear, and still align to a higher possibility, as we have been explaining, without falling into the trap that the collective consciousness has to offer.

❄

What must you do to assist in bringing about this new society? You must begin to regard all aspects of your life as an extension of the whole, as a fragment of the whole, as a piece that represents the whole, and as you regard those aspects your life, and you relate to those aspects of your life, relate to them as if they were the whole. As if they were the entire picture, as if your relationship to money, your relationship to government, your relationship to law, your relationship to all such systems reflected what is happening to the whole. For this is true. As you work on yourself, you can work on the whole. As you relate to your own life differently, you relate to the whole differently.

What does this mean? This means that you no longer regard your relationship to yourself as a fragment, but as an integral connected piece to the whole. Right now, you regard yourself as having an isolated existence. You look at your bank account, your home, your food, your body, and all of these things that make up your life as yours, separate from the whole. You do not see yourself as part of this entirely beautiful interconnected web of Light. That is the truth. You are a strand in a web of Light, and like a spider web, where one strand gets touched and it reverberates through the whole, you too can do the same by regarding your bank account as an extension of the financial system, your retirement fund as an extension of the economic system. When you pay your taxes, imagine that you are connecting with the system as a whole. When you go about your day spending money, do not think in terms of the limited exchange of money and the products you are purchasing, think instead that what you are doing is a reflection of the entire system, and do it with the intention that you are engaging in a beautiful exchange of energy, and that this exchange supports each of you—you and the person selling or buying the product—so that you are engaged in a mutual exchange of energy in support of each other.

All of these transactions can be lifted, elevated out of their ministerial and administrative and mundane existence as you now conceive of them, and instead embraced as the supportive, life-affirming gestures they are; these are the gestures of and extensions of the energy of life. This is what you are doing when you do all of these things. You are engaging in the creation and extension of life itself. Do not regard what you are doing as trivial, do not see it as mundane. See yourself in the web of life itself, as a Seed of Light, extending light through the system, to others, and them to you. As you do this, you elevate the nature of the exchange; you honor it for what it is—the extension of life to each other.

Can you look at your life and see all of the ways you are connected to the whole, and how this whole is made up of the systems that we are speaking of? In how many ways, each day, do you connect with politics, government, finances, the legal system, education? Government, law, and finance are the three domains in particular that bedevil you so much. How often are your actions involved in any or all of these? Can you regard those actions like sending light through a telephone system or electrical system, or plucking at a spider's web? See yourself in dynamic reverberation with all of it, the entire picture, and you will begin to elevate it.

How can you do this? You can regard each action you take as a form of being the Christ Consciousness, as the Christ Consciousness in action, in movement, through time and space, and in so doing you can bend the time and space around each of these domains ever so slightly. As you pay your bills, cross the street, interact with a police officer, sign a contract, make a purchase, vote, etc., you can begin to see these actions as extensions of your own self in the form of the Christ Consciousness by saying to yourself, *I am the Christ Consciousness in action as I* _____ and then fill in the blank. See it as an act of your extending the Christ Consciousness through the entire system.

Isn't this just a verbal formulation, an affirmation?

We say that this is the energy of the Christ coming through the words that you use to describe your actions as you do them, and this extends the energy through the system itself. All you need to do is imbue that act with the energy of the Christ Consciousness as you do it. It is in very small doses, but that is very different form purchasing something and saying, *I hope I got the best deal* or *I hope this doesn't break* or *I wish I didn't have to pay this bill* or *I don't really want to part with this money* or *why do I have to sit in traffic* or *why is this rule in place?*

Whenever you feel resistance toward the system, see where you fall into judgment and then act instead with the energy of the Christ Consciousness, which sees itself in dynamic creation with all other Seeds of Light. You can imbue your everyday actions with the energy of the Christ Consciousness by simply intending to do so. And yes, you can do this most powerfully by saying, *I am the Christ in action as I pay my bill. I am the Christ in action as I vote, as I file my taxes, as I save money, as I make a donation to an important cause, as I comply with this rule or this law.*

Do this and you imbue these systems with the energy of the Christ Consciousness. We promise that this is your entry point into elevating the system, into bending time and space in ways that your current efforts do not and cannot.

30

THE NEED FOR REPARATIONS

The extension of the Christ Consciousness to all aspects of your realm, to creating unity and wholeness where there is disunity and separation, to creating harmony and beauty where there is pain and disconnection, requires an additional step. We wish to expand on a topic we raised earlier by returning to the topic of reparations to the African-American community. How do you regenerate a connection between the constituent parts of your society where there is a traumatic issue, a cleavage, that occurred, as in the slavery that occurred in your country at its inception? Yes, how do you regenerate a community when that trauma is carried in the very DNA of those involved? For the trauma occurred at a cellular level and was carried and passed on from generation to generation. This is not the only example. The same can be said of the Holocaust, and there are other examples, where entire groups of people were cast aside or tortured and mistreated in profound and traumatic ways. You cannot ever hope to repair and heal this aspect of the collective consciousness simply by turning a blind eye.

No, you must begin to regenerate by *acknowledging* that energy. You have created the energy of slavery. It has a consciousness that continues to permeate throughout your society, through the society's treatment of those who are identified with a particular race. And the effect is that this trauma affects how you treat and regard each other and the ways that this difference, built around pigmentation of your skin, somehow dictates the relative worth of a person's life. And you struggle mightily with how to speak of this issue without offending, and you throw around slogans about whose lives matter, but you do not and have not yet embraced the idea that what must occur is a form of *regeneration*.

You must regenerate by repairing that which came before. The collective weight of something like slavery on the consciousness of humanity, and on the consciousness in particular of black Americans, is so pervasive, so profound, that you cannot simply sweep it under the rug.

You must recreate yourselves anew, in a new way, one that involves accepting the role you originally had in the creation of slavery, in the expansion of it, in the inscription of it at the level of language in the very document you so zealously defend, your Constitution.

Regeneration recognizes that you cannot ask any single individual to recreate themselves without the trauma and pain that an entire group of people who were subordinated and suppressed in such horrific manner as black Americans were.[1] Regeneration, then, is the *collective* effort to recreate your selves anew, in a new form, without the trauma, to recreate your selves in the now, not as you were a second ago. But when the weight of the energy is so strong, and the sweep of that energy is so wide, the consciousness of that energy is very difficult to dissipate. It is not possible for any one Seed of Light to tackle this issue alone. It is a task shared by the collective, by all of you who are part of the collective.

We have talked about co-creating each other, and being in relationship to each other. That form of co-creation has to do with an individual working with another individual, and that continues to be valid. When we are dealing with an entire structure that is deeply embedded in the collective consciousness, this is about the regeneration of the whole, and this must be dealt with by embracing the trauma by the whole. Regeneration is the healing of the whole. What happens with regeneration is that you begin to recreate and co-create each other anew in this process, with the recognition that there *is* a trauma.

Reparations acknowledge in the form of money that the trauma exists. Money is the measure of energy that you dedicate to making this a part of public consciousness. The public does not take responsibility for this now. It is complicit with the history of slavery and discrimination. You must take responsibility through reparations.

❊

White privilege has to do with how you co-create each other and allow certain Seeds of Light to be complicit with this without taking responsibility for it or even acknowledging it. That means that you all share in the co-creation of this energy of trauma that began so many years ago and has grown, because it is reproduced but not consciously acknowledged in a way that would allow for forgiveness. Regeneration is the process of collective forgiveness for a trauma so large that it engulfs an entire population. That is the issue of slavery and discrimination here—that you have engulfed each other, the entire population, in an original trauma, and this energy is produced and reproduced again and again in myriad forms, and it now has a life of its own.

Regeneration is where you begin to tackle this on a collective scale. It is healing on a collective scale. You know how difficult it is to heal and eliminate your pain and suffering on an individual scale, because the energy you have created is created again and again and then has a life of its own and persists. It has its own consciousness, is part of consciousness, and resists elimination. It wishes to reproduce itself.[2] The same is true of collective trauma, but on a much larger scale.

Reparation is the means by which you begin to take conscious action to reproduce yourselves anew, to resurrect yourself as a collective, whole and untarnished by the collective trauma that originated so many years ago and which has shaped and defined your co-creation of each other. It is a part of the collective consciousness, and this is what must be undone. Reparation is the means by which you go back and lay the foundation for rebirth as a whole, as a new collective. No one person can do this. The trauma is too great. The energy of the trauma has a consciousness too powerful and too deeply rooted in the collective consciousness for any one person to extract themselves from it. They are inevitably shaped by it, even if they are not conscious of it. This is, as we said, the reason that white privilege is so powerful, because you are partaking of an energy of trauma that shapes you as much as it shapes others, and yet you do not realize how it shapes you.

Reparation is the step of recognition of your involvement in and complicity with the energy of the original trauma, and it is equally important for you to acknowledge this as it is for those who have been harmed to be willing to forgive and resurrect themselves anew. This collective rebirth requires that reparations be made so that the collective energy of the trauma can be released. That is what must be done on a collective, national scale here in your country in order to move beyond the effects of that trauma, which persist in all of these areas that we have been discussing—education, politics, economics, and the judicial system. All of it is infused with the collective energy of the trauma of slavery and discrimination in your country, and without this step, which is the critical regeneration of yourselves together as a whole, you will not ascend, no, you will not ascend.

The ascension of humanity depends upon the relinquishing of the trauma of separation built upon the difference you call race. That you have done such untold harm to each other and on the basis of what you call race, on the basis of skin coloring and certain features, is madness, utter and complete madness from our perspective. The Christ Consciousness sees all individuals, all of you, as equally divine and recognizes your divinity regardless of form. That is the truth. *Regardless of form.* And so this trauma is the major critical step that is facing this particular nation. And each nation has its own version at the core of the nation's own history.

The transcendence of race and the transcendence of the nation as constructs of the collective consciousness, which will give way to the unity consciousness of the globe, to the Christ Consciousness that sees all as equal in every way, requires that this stage of reparation and regeneration take place. And so you must all begin to see where you are in alignment and agreement with the structural racism and discrimination that infiltrate your society and begin to make reparations.

As we have said, the monetary reparations that must be made are not the solution alone. No, they are a measure of your willingness to repair the past by recreating each other anew and addressing the issue by making it part of the collective discussion, the willingness to acknowledge and say that this is how you have co-created each other for so long. That is why reparations are necessary. Otherwise, the traumatic energy will persist and emerge in other forms and continue to grow as it has.

✳

There is an understanding among you that when you repair and offer reparations you are basically setting the scales even. This is not what is happening. It cannot happen. You cannot possibly set the scales even. That is itself an image and a byproduct of the collective consciousness—that the idea of punishment or reparation somehow sets scales of justice in balance. This continues to see some of you as wrongdoers who must be punished and somehow make the other—the black community—whole again. And it keeps you each separate. This is not an image that the Christ Consciousness holds for the outcome of reparation and regeneration. No, this is not the image.

The reason is that those who were enslaved and discriminated against were never *not* whole. They were always in a state of utter perfection, as divine beings. It could not be otherwise. That they suffered tremendously and continue to suffer now cannot be denied. This is not a denial. This is to say that their status as whole, complete, and perfect creations in the eyes of the Light, in the eyes of the Creator, cannot in any way be ignored.

Those who do not want to pay for reparations say that they are not responsible—they did not engage in slavery. And we have said elsewhere that you are responsible for the whole. So no, this is not the purpose of reparations and regeneration, which suggests taking from one as punishment to make the other whole. No, the purpose and the image we wish to convey is understanding that the persons who were harmed were always whole, always deserved all that life has to offer, and for those who are now engaged in the practice of healing this at a societal level, the efforts made are not to repay any one person, nor to punish you. They are the means by which you begin to acknowledge that the systems that have built up around you—as a result of this traumatic energy that has been created and recreated and deepened throughout your nation's history—have inflicted real wounds. And reparations are simply the first step in undermining that systemic harm. It is the conscious and concrete means of acknowledging your need to regenerate your relationships, your entire concept of what it means to be human and to share this earth together. Yes, that is what *reparation* means.

The exchange of money, as we have explained, is the way in which you transfer energy that moves and exchanges form; it is the power to move and create through energy, specifically, through energy that has taken form. You spend and receive money, and you are able to purchase and buy objects, things, etc. And you inhabit a world, you have created a world, in which material reality has not been accessible to many because of the systemic constructs you have built on the foundation of separation known as racism, in which you have demeaned and dehumanized generations of people based on the construct you call race.

Thus, the reparation is also important for it is the exchange of energy that allows for the acquisition and movement of form, of material objects, and that has been an important part of how the lives of those impacted by your society's discrimination have suffered. It is but one aspect, but the reparation makes it apparent; it acknowledges it. It is part of a larger path toward regeneration, which encompasses other aspects, many of which we have already taught you, such as forgiveness.[3]

But our point is that the end result is not the balancing of scales, not so that you are on equal footing in the eyes of justice, so that one's pain is now balanced out and you are each now equal, because one has paid the other. No, you were always whole and perfect, and the misguided energy that inflicted discrimination upon some of you did not detract from that, but it did create a world in which you were constantly told that you were not equal, that you were not whole. One of the primary ways that it has played out is the absence of access to the material forms of this realm, in the form of housing or possessions or jobs. The proper step for divine order to be restored is an acknowledgement that your fellow Seeds of Light were deprived of full access to this material realm. Reparation is your way of acknowledging this denial of access and beginning the process of regeneration.

31

EMBRACING CHANGE

*I*t is vitally important that you understand that your role in shaping in this new society is not fixed. It is not one that requires you to be or play a certain role. You do not have to be in politics, to be in finance, or be a healer, or whatever you think is required for you to be able to shape this new society. It happens through your everyday interactions. It happens through the way you remain complicit with and in agreement with and even in alignment with the system as it currently exists. So you do not need to run for office or try to occupy one of the positions you think needs changing in order to bring about social change.

You can do that, but understand that you are also likely to run into barriers that will lead you to be the same as you were, to act in a way consistent with the collective consciousness. As you continue in your life, as you deepen your connection with your own true, divine nature, the important task before you is to be mindful of when you fall back into alignment with the collective consciousness, particularly at the societal or global level. That is, when you are engaging in an area where you feel powerless, where you feel that you cannot make any changes alone, it is your mindset that you can control, that you *must* control, as you begin to relate to all of these areas differently. That is where you deny your power, where you deny your role as a co-creator of this realm.

It is most important that you release the belief that you are not co-creating this system. You have the power to change it without embracing the normal and ordinary paths to change that you know so well. Yes, if you wish to run for office or start a campaign or do something that puts you in the public eye, do so, but be prepared to confront the collective will, the collective consciousness of those who are not ready for change and who don't even know that they are co-creators of this realm. You must be prepared for that too, or you will fall into older patterns.

What you can do—and we have said this, but it bears repeating—is engage wherever you can in the ways that allow you to speak as a Seed of Light. Not necessarily in those words, not in the vocabulary that we are using. But understand where you can enact and co-create as the Christ Consciousness with love, forgiveness, and compassion, where there is no separation. Unity is the voice that you must embrace. So as you relate to these systems, remember to invoke the Christ Consciousness—*I am the Christ Consciousness in this realm. I am the Christ Consciousness in the world of politics, banking, finance, the law, etc.* Wherever you are, remember to invoke and be the Christ Consciousness, to take your action with the intention, to imbue your action and words with the Light of the Christ Consciousness by being conscious that you are co-creating in that very moment. That is, of course, all there is at that very moment.

And when you hand over your money or vote or watch the news or do anything that connects you with these systems, invoke the Christ Consciousness in your thoughts and in your body. You must embody the feeling of love, unity, and forgiveness. That is how you begin to bend space and time around these institutions, around these structures of thought. We emphasize this because the feeling of powerlessness, the feeling that the structure is too big, or that it is not important and does not affect you and you are not a part of it, are all ways of diminishing your creative power, of denying your status as a spark of the Creator itself.

❋

The same approach must be taken with your system of money, which is already in flux. The very energy you use to exchange material form in a material world is undergoing a transformation. This is not a trivial shift.

You have something called Bitcoin, and this is a currency unlike your current system of currency. Bitcoin is where you are learning that the energy you create that allows for the movement of goods and services is tied to your sense of an agreement of what it means. And this was always inherent in your systems and how you valued money, and had exchange rates and so all sorts of ways of addressing the flow of money that are little more than conventions. Money increases or decreases in value according to changes that are nothing more than a reflection of your emotional state and your agreed-upon system of currency.

The same also exists with this new creation, this idea of using some other system to reflect how you value objects. This is not tethered to what you used to use—the gold standard, which was that you would take a precious metal, the object known as gold, and then value that according to some paper note that somehow stood in for that object, and that object stood in for something else. And now you have moved away from a precious object to a precious paper object, and now to electronic objects, where your money circulates entirely in the realm of the word. You use numbers and send information back and forth, but these are just pieces and bits of information, in language, that you now used to transfer and ship goods and services.

Why is this important?

It has to do with the nature and value of your current monetary system and how it is in flux, how it is changing. You must understand the role that money plays in your entire system, and this is an integral part of that understanding. Understand that the system is destabilizing from its current form, and all the efforts you make to control how money is valued are changing, and you see all sorts of problems in the world with that valuation. You can see how your efforts to control the value of goods by how much you impose taxes and tariffs on goods coming into a country are not working.

What we want you to understand is that as you progress toward a new society, the rules around the creation of money and the agreements you currently have are beginning to break, they are beginning to be disrupted, and so alternative systems like Bitcoin are emerging. This other currency is something else, some other way of valuing, and you will soon learn that people can simply agree—*I have so many coins, and I want this object or this service,* and you agree collectively that this service is worth so many coins. Maybe initially you start off with one currency, a currency in the current system, that you all recognize, and then there's an exchange of value between the new currency and the old currency, with some sense of how many Bitcoins is the equivalent of a dollar. And then you might begin to operate in this new currency, without any regard to the old currency. Then the old currency goes away, and there's no physical money anymore, and you have a whole new system where the valuation takes place by agreement and you simply shift numbers back and forth. Your own goods and services can be worth a certain number of Bitcoins, and someone will pay you in that new currency. And you will then spend that currency to obtain other goods and services, without any reference to a prior currency. This happened with the Euro, and many other prior currencies fell by the wayside.

The point is to illuminate your approach to this destabilization and shift around money, in more than just the typical terms of abundance that you often use. Much of your talk around money is in terms of being open to it, and receiving it, and being abundant, and therefore having your material needs met. And this we applaud; there is nothing wrong with having your material needs met. But you often avoid a more detailed understanding of the monetary system, and the arrival of the Christ Consciousness means that you must begin to understand the flow of money in a way that you do not, so that you do not fall back into the collective consciousness or your old patterns of behavior as the world monetary systems shift. This means you must begin to deepen your knowledge of money, all of you, and how it currently works, so that you do not react to

changes with fear, with resentment, with some sort of disbelief—or simply ignore those changes.

For the world economy to shift in the light of the Christ
Consciousness means you must be invested, literally and figu-
ratively, in the world's economy. You must bring your Light to
that economy through your knowledge of an interaction with
that system. You cannot simply sit and ask for more money and
hope that it arrives. You cannot remain in the same patterns of
opening to abundance. There is nothing wrong with this. You
deserve abundance.

But, again, the issue is that the world around you is shifting;
it is changing. These shifts will become even greater for the new
world order built on the Christ Consciousness to emerge. For
there to be unity and inclusivity, you must be part of the creation of this new world economy. Do not hide from the issue of
money because it may scare you, or because of your belief that
the shifts are beyond your control or, worse still, because you
still harbor some sort of resentment or disdain toward money,
toward the energy that moves the physical and material realm.
That is a mistake, for as you occupy this realm, you cannot ignore the system of monetary exchange that allows you to survive here.

✳

The process by which you will bring this new society into creation, into manifestation, into form, is not going to be *easy* in
the sense of that word as you understand it. It is not a seamless
path by which you simply show up and in consensus say, *We are
the Christ Consciousness and we are now going to live in harmony*

and unity! No, this is a process by which many, many lives will continue to unfold within the strictures of the collective consciousness, and will continue to bear the trauma of separation.

This is not a process that happens by what you call referendum, where you all just agree with a collective vote to be in unison, to become one voice. No, each of you is still an individual Seed of Light, working toward your own unity with the Divine, with the Creator of all, and you will still need to learn your karmic lessons.

Does that mean this place will never be the kind of heaven we imagine it could be?

Yes and no, and this is a critical point. For you all imagine, with some sort of creative vision in your mind, what the world would look like in unison. It is a kind of diffuse image, nothing too specific, and in it you imagine a kind of vague happiness where you are all just happy all the time, hugging each other and blissful, as if there were just one big endless party. That's the kind of image you have of what society would look like, and we are not going to tell you that it's wrong, only that it wouldn't look like that if you were to see it now. In some respects, the world might look the same to you, and to others it would look dramatically different. Yes, we understand the conundrum. You ask, *How could it look the same if we are all in unity consciousness? Would there be judges or prisons or would we have any fights or squabbling? What would that seem like? And if we did have that kind of stuff, does that mean we haven't achieved unity?*

This is what we can tell you: If you were united, you would not have a world where poverty is rampant, where people's self-worth is tied to their identity and where they have a need to fight for it. You would not have a world where the earth's resources are squandered and ignored, with the effects dumped on future generations. You would not have rampant discrepancies in wealth. You would not see entire generations of individuals incarcerated based on the most trivial of acts. There are so many things that would change. But you would all still be living in human bodies and working through your abilities to be with each other in perfect harmony. There are aspects to being separate that would still entail the transfer of material goods from place to place, in time and space, for this is the arena in which you are created and must still navigate. Those aspects would not cease.

But the most fundamental change of all is that you would not be in disagreement with each other over the value of who you are and what you really are. Your interactions would always begin with a baseline of compassion, love, and respect for the fullness and potential of the other person. Your primary emotional question would not be, *What does this mean for me?* It would be something else, something rooted in your support for the collective, knowing that the collective supports you for you are one.

Understand that this is available to you now, in the way in which you relate to what is happening around you, for everything around you is a creation of love, in love, and cannot be otherwise, for that is what the entire universe is created of. It is made of love and only love, taking the form in which you as co-creators of the universe make it to be. So you can now relate to it as love, even as you see it taking forms that do not inspire love and seem entirely antithetical to love. You can see the ways in which the very energy of the universe is shaped and molded to become what you experience. It is still love at its core. And so you would relate to the world, even if it appears to be the same, from an entirely different consciousness that would not see everything as a threat to survival and require you to separate yourself and defend yourself. You would still have streets and places to live, and beds to sleep on, and you would still eat and drink, and you would still talk to each other and exchange thoughts.

For you understand that the movement back to unity requires separation in the first instance. That is why there is time and space. That is the agreement you have made with each other to experience reality as it appears to you now. But it would be experienced by you differently, and then as a result of that experience, time and space bend, and newer forms are created. And how you experience those forms is different, each instance moving away from separation and toward love and unity. This is the meaning of the Christ Consciousness at the level of society. You will experience society's movements in the same way as you experience the physical world around you. It is in constant motion and flux, moving as all of you co-create each other again and again in each instant, in each moment of time, according to your shared agreements at the level of consciousness.

So you will slowly but surely see—as you all relate to society at large differently—that society will shift. It always has. That is the history of your civilization as you have documented it already, going back to ancient cultures. Those societies bear little resemblance to yours, except for one fundamental fact: You were all driven by separation. And that is what is changing, and we cannot dictate to you to how it will look, because how it looks will depend on your ability to relate to it and experience it from a place of wholeness and unity, not from separation. To paint the picture now, looking at it from a place of separation, would in fact not make sense. You will see an incomplete picture and you would relate to it from a state of separation. It will not seem like the perfect creation that it is.

32

THE TASK OF UNITING HUMANITY

*A*s we approach the end of this volume, many questions arise. *How will we get there? What will it look like? Who else needs to be involved? Don't we need everyone to wake up? Is this even possible?* Yes, these are all important questions *for your mind.* Yes, for your mind to ask. For you imagine creating society like something you would plan, a project that you would sit down together and outline, like it was a school project or a term paper, or something like that. Yes, you would just map it out.

But isn't there some need to proceed consciously, so that we don't just replicate?

Yes, but planning something and trying to get there by normal means will not work. It doesn't happen that way. You are led, and you end up somewhere you didn't realize you could be, by virtue of stepping each time more fully into yourself. Imagine that it is more like a path, where the next step lights up as you need to take it. You can't see the entire way, no, you can't. For if you could, you would think, *I know a better way to get there. We can make a short-cut here or go this way.* Or you would start trying to build something that isn't yet ready to be built. Understand that your task is not to set out and lay forth in a blueprint what this new society will look like, with the tasks that are to be assigned to each person.

No, your task is to align to its possibility, and to be the Christ Consciousness in all areas of your life and in these systems. That is your goal and your task as you learn to co-create differently your own relationship to these areas. Does this mean you cannot speak, that you cannot rally others? No, it does not, but understand that others will not approach this as you will, from the perspective of the Christ Consciousness, if they are not ready, if they have not awoken.

And that is why you cannot plan, for you would amass a set of people who are not ready to relate to these systems in the same way. The collective consciousness into which they are absorbed would bubble up and that is what you would reproduce, consciously. But as you speak and engage, you must speak and engage from a place of compassion, forgiveness, and unity. Those are the marks of the Christ Consciousness. Meeting people where they are, not reproducing them as in the past, not expecting them to be different or judging them for being different, but aligning to their higher possibility, seeing their full divinity before they have, and remembering that you are all co-creating together, as Seeds of Light, as slivers of the Creator itself.

As we come to a close, there is a key message we wish to impart as you embark on this phase of reproducing your society anew in the light of the Christ Consciousness: Whatever you *think* it looks like, that is not it. It will always look different from your expectations. Do not impose your vision on the future, for you will attempt to steer the manifestation. Open to the *feeling* of what the future looks like, how it inspires you, and do not allow the images of what you think the world should look like to dictate how you react. That is the fundamental message. So do not begin to think that money will disappear or fall from trees, or that you will no longer have politicians at all, but something else like some master computer that runs the show. No, the point is not for you to conjure mentally a new future, a new society, but to align to the feeling of connection and unity and wonder created by the possibility of a society formed out of the Christ Consciousness.

❋

You understand that your task, all of you, is to invoke the Christ Consciousness in all areas of your lives. In this volume we have been addressing what it means to invoke the Christ Consciousness at the level of your society, in the realm of your institutions and structures that have been built up to deal with your separation. We have been addressing your systems of governance, law, and finance, that is, how you govern and control each other, how you exchange the energy in your realm necessary for the movement of material goods and services, and how you handle those who do not conform to the rules that your society has put down. This is how you manage separation all the time, through these systems of governance, and we have touched on other aspects of your system such as the education system, which inculcates and absorbs you into these systems and structures.

This is where we come to a close, for we have touched on so many aspects of your society, yet in broad strokes, for it is you who must invoke the Christ Consciousness—*you*. We wish to come back to some basic principles and address the difficulties you face in transforming your social structures because they seem so powerful and so dominant. For many of you, fear and acquiescence may seem far more inviting approaches to what is surely a daunting task.

We have stressed that the transformation of your society will not take place in your lifetime, but this not the means by which you must measure your effect. This is a critical area for so many of you, for you evaluate your efforts by whether you can measure success or failure, by whether you can discern effects at all. This is understandable. You engage in some action or behavior and you wish to see the energetic reverberations in the rest of the collective consciousness. If nothing appears to happen, you think that nothing *has* happened. That is, you wait for the energetic reverberation to manifest in your life in some concrete way or by a response from someone else.

But this not how you must look at this work. No, this work transcends your lifetime, and for that reason, you cannot fall prey to the temptation to say, *Nothing is changing, so let's go back to our old ways. Let's rally and fight and cry, and kick out the old politicians and just change everything all at once. Let's do this in the course of a single election cycle*—or however long you are willing to go before you decide that nothing has changed still, and that you need a new onslaught of change.

This is not going to produce the results you think it is. No, it is not. For instead, you will fall back into the old paradigms of opposition and rebellion against something else. You will replicate another binary, and you will simply entrench the collective consciousness of separation further in the minds of those with whom you are in contact. Yes, you and your fellow Seeds of Light will continue to reproduce each other as you have already known each other, instead of aligning with the possibility of something new, a new paradigm for change. There are already murmurings of this change occurring in small ways throughout your society, and it is important that you remain attuned to them, and become aware of them, and spread them, because that is the sign of change.

Change may not be immediate, it may not yet be anything more than skin deep, to use a different analogy, but those changes are occurring. You must nurture them, elaborate on them, deepen them by aligning to these possibilities and others, and by aligning to the possibility of transformation where exclusion, greed, fighting, and winning are not the dominant modes of engagement. No, you must continue to operate from perspectives of compassion, forgiveness, and unity. The ways of the past, which simply reiterate a person's sense of separation from the rest of the world, are never going to achieve the goals of justice or rehabilitation or integration. Whether that is incarcerating large numbers of people, or allowing multi-million dollar corporations to continue to amass wealth and use it to determine the political fates of those who seek office, or continuing behaviors that allow a few to access many of the resources available to you now while the majority cannot.

You will, at every turn, wish to turn back and fight and cajole and push and prod and do all manner of things to see that there is change. Yet you cannot do this. We have shown you how. We have told you how to relate to the systems and what intention to have when you engage with them, and what verbal formulations to use whenever you encounter these systems and the aspects of them rooted in separation trigger a vehement and angry reaction in you.

Yes, there has been injustice. Yes, there has been discrimination. Yes, there has been enormous suffering and pain. None of this is to be denied. But neither is it the source of your response, in the sense that you simply seek justice or an eye-for-an-eye or to set the scales even or that you must assume that the system will always look like this. No, none of that is the case. And it is in the face of such a daunting task that you must continue to reiterate your allegiance to the Christ Consciousness as the vehicle for change in your life, and in the life of your entire society.

You can, of course, always invoke the Christ Consciousness verbally, you can always say, *I am the Christ Consciousness in and through [this situation]*. Yes, it is that simple. There are other verbal formulations we have given you, but this a simple means of reminding yourself that you are always in connection with the Christ Consciousness as vehicle for emancipation, as a means of undoing the separation between you and others and that allows you to transcend the limits of time and space as you known them currently.

By connecting with the Christ Consciousness, by invoking it, through your willingness to meet everyone with compassion, to align to a possibility for a future society where separation is not the foundation for all of your systems, you will be invoking the energy of the Christ Consciousness again and again. And just like the murmurings for change that you have begun to see in your society, many more will come. So remember this when you feel frustrated and feel that society isn't changing, isn't getting any better, or perhaps even looks worse. Remember that the effects of your actions transcend your lifetime, and their ripple effect will be felt for generations to come. The energy that you put out will have its own consciousness, the consciousness of the Christ, and that energy will seek to grow and expand, and you will soon be inviting other Seeds of Light, who see themselves in you, in your modeling of the Christ Consciousness, and they too will begin to awaken and perform the same role for others. It is the way. It is already written. It is the will of the Creator.

※

You must remember, all of you, that as you assume your task to create this new world, and you begin to align with a new society, the possibility of which remains in your grasp but is not yet manifest, you must be vigilant not to assume that you know what it must look like even as you see it unfolding, for it will not resemble what you expect it to be now. No, it will resemble something else entirely, nothing that you have preconceived. This is critical, which is why we repeat this point, for it is your tendency to want to visualize and predict and prepare to chart out a course to reach this future. You inevitably drag with you parts of the past, parts that you may not even be aware of, that come from and are rooted in the collective consciousness. You must be open, and constantly be willing to drop what you know, to drop what you know and be like a blank slate.

What might this look like? You can ask and invite this to emerge, to come forward, and this will be what you encounter what you co-create in the realm of the possible, in the realm of receptivity, not in the realm of planning and mapping out a blueprint. You are encountering a new way of manifesting and co-creating, as you open to more possibilities than have ever existed in this realm, and you cannot try to duplicate what came before, for this has been your path and your way for millennia. It is now time to open to a new way of doing and a new way of being. Being led and allowing the possibilities that you are not aware of to emerge, for you to learn and see anew.

And, no, this does not mean you won't end up replicating. That is inevitable. But it means that when you realize you are replicating, when you are dragging the past with you, you will see it and ask, *What else is there? What other possibilities are there?* And not everything from the past is unusable or must be discarded. It is only that you cannot possibly know precisely what is and isn't right for this new future, for a society grounded in inclusivity and forgiveness and compassion. So it is your humility and willingness to relinquish the sense that you know, that you have the answer—that must be your touchstone as you see and watch as new structures emerge and grow. Those too will evolve and change, and they will become closer and closer to what needs to be so that the world can come into full unity with the Christ Consciousness. That is all you need to do and know at this moment.

Yes, this requires an enormous amount of trust and a willingness to forego outcomes and the certainty that you know you are doing it right. Yes, this is another way of doing things, and of being in your realm, which you have not much experience practicing. So too will you learn to practice this way of allowing life to emerge. And when it does, you will see that the structures you need are far simpler, and far more readily capable of handling the kinds of exigencies that emerge in any human relationship.

As you move from separation to unity, you will inevitably experience and encounter setbacks. And by *setbacks* we only mean those moments of rupture, where exclusivity and separation will again govern, even if for a brief moment, your interactions with others, and with your fellow society. That is okay. There is never going to be a perfect alignment all at once. There will be a slow evolution toward this unity, and we have stressed that you will not experience this in your lifetime. And that too is okay.

We will close today by stressing that there is one thing that you must be willing to do, in addition to all that we have said, and that is to accept your own death. Yes, you must be willing to accept your own death. For you recognize that much of what you have been dealing with, and what we have touched on throughout these books, is your inability to face your own death.[1] You must face the fact that your physical form will be returned to the earth, and will become material once again that forms part of this earth. Just as you came from the earth, and the earth has sustained you, along with the sun, you will return to those elements, and your life force will move onto a different plane.

It is your willingness to accept your death that allows you to embrace the Christ Consciousness fully, for when you have acknowledged the loss of physical form, to have truly accepted and embraced this and as a fundamental truth of your existence here and released the fear that so often accompanies it, then the ability to align with the frequency of the Christ Consciousness becomes unquestionable. You cannot but align to the Christ Consciousness, for when that fear of death has been accepted, you are in full alignment with life, and that is all the Christ Consciousness really is. It is the life force itself that runs through all of you, and through all living beings, including the earth and its animals and other inhabitants.

And so you will be filled with life and be willing to see all of life as this beautiful dance and flow of energy. It becomes easy then to see that the monumental efforts you perceive as necessary to reform your society are just a very small part of the entire life cycle of all of life, of this entire realm. You will open to the forgiveness and compassion that you truly are as you encounter these seemingly entrenched systems of your society. And this will allow you to move through them with grace and ease. It will allow you to bring the Seed of Light that you are to bear on those structures, in the ways that we have taught you here and in our previous teachings, so that the world can transform in the way that is already written. You are the Christ, you have arisen. May all of you awaken to the power and frequency of the Christ Consciousness. May all of you open into the fullness of who you truly are: divine Seeds of Light in human form.

33

COURAGE IN THE FACE
OF RESISTANCE

We wish to close today with gifts for those of you willing and courageous enough to take on the task of embracing the Christ Consciousness and embodying it in this realm. That is no easy task, no easy task at all, for you invite all sorts of criticism and reproach, and this will indeed trigger many aspects of your selves that still are being released and that you have yet to encounter. You will soon discover that you are now entirely immersed in the soup of the collective consciousness, and that you cannot escape it. Not in the way that you often think of escaping it.

To be in *agreement* with it but not in *alignment* with it is actually the most difficult task you can take upon yourself. For it means to be aware, deeply aware, of the systems of thought and the ways of thinking that you have now dismantled in yourself. You see them, and you could fall easily back into them, but you will not. But you will find that it is not the case that you simply float through life as if there were nothing to worry about. This is not the type of ascension that many of you imagine, where you sort of float through the world of physical form as if you were not a part of it, somehow magically able to manipulate it and control it, like you were in some sort of fantasy realm, with special powers. The fact that you understand the construction of reality in and through space and time, as a collective endeavor, does not mean that you escape the co-creation that you undertake with your fellow Seeds of Light.

You must understand that there will be resistance, in you and others, and that this resistance cannot be met in the same way as you would have in the past, with pushing and prodding and cajoling and fighting and arguing. No, for that resistance is the moment in which you fall back into the old paradigm. But understand too that this resistance will emerge in you, and you will find yourself wondering about the place you occupy in this realm, and what you can do if you are truly, authentically yourself, if you embrace fully your nature as a Seed of Light, if you accept that you are co-creating the world in this very moment. Many will condemn you, as this is not a teaching that many accept. It does not comport with that their eyes tell them, and it certainly does not comport with their beliefs about the nature of reality, even if those beliefs also don't line up with what their eyes tell them.

So many will object to the notion that there is a Christ Consciousness that you all share, or that it can in some ways be the vehicle for massive social change. This will come most often from those who have an investment in the figure of the Christ as he has been presented for millennia. For the idea that you are all the Christ, that you are all co-creating with the gift of the

Creator, with the Light that you are, is anathema to those who believe that there is a one and only Christ who must be revered like an idol whose love only some of you can attain. You will be met with resistance, and much worse, by those who feel threatened by the very notion that you can have a direct relationship with the Creator. That you are in fact already directly connected with the Creator, with all of life, and that you are somehow on equal footing with and equally divine as the figure who has been elevated and exalted in some form of religious institution.

To believe that you are the Christ Consciousness and that you are all reshaping society at each and every moment is not blasphemy, it is not idolatry, it is not grandiosity. It is the truth. But the truth has often been the source of a great animosity and strife among humans, who are driven by their need to control and by their hunger for power. So you must be prepared for the idea that your life is not necessarily going to improve in all respects when you embrace the path of co-creating society in and through the Christ Consciousness. That is okay, but many are not fully prepared for what this means. Some of you may lose friends and family, others may lose jobs or feel that they can no longer circulate in certain social settings. And still others may find themselves surprised at where they can be authentically the Christ incarnate, in human form.

All you can do is meet people where they are, understand that you are co-creating each other at this very moment, and with the power of forgiveness, compassion, and empathy, you can bend time and space to call forth the fullness of every being you meet. It is an enormous undertaking that you are embarking on, a powerful and courageous journey of bringing down so much more Light than this world has ever experienced. To say that you are courageous is an understatement. To say that you are miraculous would be more accurate. Yes, you are a miracle made flesh, all of you, and as we come to a close, with just one more installment, we express our love and support for you as you embark on this journey, on this adventure, in calling in the Christ Consciousness to reshape your society.

❄

As we bring this series of works to a close, we remind you that the words of this work and our prior works bring you closer to the Christ Consciousness. Yes, our words are little Seeds of Light, capsules of energy that when you are ready, open you further and further to the energy of and frequency of the Christ Consciousness. As you read and reread, you will continue to open and deepen. As you practice the various verbal formulations we have given you for invoking the Light, for invoking the Christ Consciousness, you will align yourself more and more. Each time you will resurrect yourself in a new wavelength, in a new frequency of Light, that comes closer and closer to the Christ Consciousness, to the frequency of unconditional love, forgiveness, and compassion. It is the frequency of the Creator. It is the truth of who you really are. And so we wish to close by offering you one last formulation, one last way to invoke the Christ: *I am the Christ in all I see before me, now and forever, past, present, and future. I am the Christ in all I see before me.*

You are the Christ in physical form. You are the Christ embodied. We love and bless you all as you fulfill your soul's duty in bringing about the ascension of the planet, and co-creating a new realm on the earth.

CONCLUSION

A s you ascend and embark on this new journey together, as you all face the darkness that you have yourselves created and manifested in this realm, as co-creators, as the Seeds of Light, as the slivers of the Creator that you are, you are embarking on a tremendously difficult journey. This is a time of incredible change, and you are not all ready for the journey in the sense that many of you will seek to return to the past, will fall into nostalgia, will choose a version of the world, of life, that you already know and that no longer exists. This is not the way. The way of nostalgia is always an effort to create something that can no longer be created, that has lived and fulfilled its purpose, and so you are attempting to recreate a paradigm that can no longer serve you. That is why you ultimately find all nostalgia unfulfilling, for it only satisfies something, a craving for something familiar, for safety and security, when you are actually being called by the world, by the universe, to grow and extend into realms and ways of being that you have never experienced. This is the power of the new, the now, the novelty of that which has yet to unfold before you.

Do not be afraid, do not fear what it is to come, even though it will ask more of you than you have ever been asked, for you are now embarking on a tremendous path of acceleration, of ascension, of moving beyond the paradigms that separate you and that have set forth the terms by which you can claim existence, by which you can live in this world. Those are dissolving, and they are not to be recreated. As you create something anew, your old creations, the creations of patriarchy and identity politics, are falling by the wayside. Yes, you are moving toward unity. That means the flimsy architecture that you have built to support yourselves, to support your subjectivity, now must be dismantled. That entity will not go softly into the night, as you like to say, for it is exists and wishes to hold onto itself.

Be strong. Be courageous. You are always loved and supported by the universe, by the Light, by all that is, for you are a part of this very matrix, this entire web of Light that is the universe, the living, breathing, knowing universe. You can call it God, the Light, or the Universe. It matters not to the Light. All that matters is that you are part of it, and you are loved, so loved, loved beyond your imagination, beyond all possible permutations of love that you have conjured for yourselves as humans. Trust that you are loved and guided, and as the darkness falls around you, do not feel afraid, do not try to dispel the darkness through anger or blame or judgment. That is not the way. Shine ever brighter, with the power of forgiveness, compassion, and rebirth that are your gifts as the Christ Consciousness. These are your gifts; they are your powers. Shine ever brighter, and illuminate the path for others, no matter how much they wish to turn to the past, to point fingers and blame.

They know no another way.

That is your purpose. Those who hold this book in their hands are there to show the way, to light the path to a new society, to a new collective consciousness. That is your mission and purpose in life. Be the Light. Be the Christ. Be love.

WHY EVERYTHING IS FALLING APART AND IT'S OKAY

*O*ver two years have passed since our original transmission,[1] and during this time, you have encountered many changes in your political, legal, and financial systems. And yet little has been transformed. You are in the midst of great upheaval. Your President no longer believes in hiding his true motives, nor do many other politicians, who are transparent in their grasp for power. And so you see what happens when a form of consciousness is being pulled away—it resists. You are witnessing the resistance of an older form of consciousness dying, and it is a slow and agonizing process for all of you to watch and witness and experience. You are in the throes of it, and it will last for some time. Even if you manage to install someone new, you will not be done with this process, for this process is not limited to one person, one party, or one period in your democracy or in any of the other structures you have.

For again, you resort to thinking of this as a kind of bad apple problem in which one person, who is symptomatic of the issue, is removed, and then you find yourself wondering why that change has not led to the emancipation or equality or justice or whatever other value you are beholden to. No, that is not what happens. Each is just a manifestation of a particular vibration of that consciousness. It is being removed, it is being transformed, but that takes time, for so many of you are still a part of it, still asking yourselves the same questions, still relating to each other through the lens of judgment and separation. And it is almost more difficult, for you once you find yourselves making changes that you regard as positive, you slip into that framework, because change gives you the perception that all is being set right, and that you don't have to make the effort ask the questions or do anything else to usher in a new era.

Do not be persuaded by this line of thinking. Do not believe that you are failing to transform this world if a conservative candidate is chosen instead of a new progressive candidate. Nor do we say that it is better to have a conservative candidate win. No, we do not. We understand that the progressive candidates in your midst champion the rights and values of many who are not given voices, and this is to be applauded. Rather, we want you to know that the selection of one over the other is not evidence that a shift has happened. It is not evidence that a "war" is being won.

This is the wrong way to view what is happening, and that is what we must impress upon all of you—to be aware of your attitude as you perceive the changes in your society. For you fluctuate constantly, up and down, angry and elated, with every little move. You perceive each shift as some sort of indication of a front between two sides, and the movement back and forth between two halves, the right side and the wrong side, and it is this thinking that must be abandoned if you are to usher in an enlightened society. You cannot do so if you regard each instance as a victory or a loss. You cannot regard each and every vote, trial, or decision as going into one column or another, or that balance emerges from there, with one side having "more" than the other. Do you not see the fundamental flaw in this outlook? In this view of the world as a kind of balance sheet? No, you cannot win this war. You have to recognize that there is no winning; there is no war. There is only loving your brethren, your fellow humans, as perfect manifestations of their divinity, even if their words and actions betray that divinity, for they do not know the truth of who they are. That is your task: to remind them always of their truth. And this is no easy task.

Does that mean that we abandon the pursuit of justice, like not investigating wrongdoing by one party or by the President?

We do not mean this at all. We mean only that you do not regard the *outcome* as meaning that you've won or lost in some "battle" for justice. That the President is punished and imprisoned or simply removed from office or pardoned or exonerated are not indications of whether one side is "winning" or "losing." This is your artificial imposition of a matrix onto the events as you perceive them. It is you who sees the world this way, and that is the very perception that must be altered by recognizing that there is no opposition to be had. Yes, there is the vibration of fear, of scarcity, the anger and resentment of others. But do not match it, do not meet with it your own form of fear and anger and resentment and disillusion. For that is all you have managed to create then. You have managed to allow one form of creation to beget another form of creation, all of it mired in the lowest energetic forms.

Each of you must learn to see the world as a divine creation, as a world filled with love and magic, where what you are seeing is simply the collective manifestation of your minds all working together to create this playground in which you all dance as Light and shadow, and you are asked to see it all as Light.

Embrace each other, as you would your own child. That is what you must do. And it is one of the hardest feats you can accomplish. Do you realize how hard it is for you to simply accept each other as each other? It is the simplest task, and requires no action on your part. The mere act of accepting each other, of giving each other full permission to exist, without any judgment or expectation or imposition or demand or challenge. Can you image what it would be like to allow each other full autonomy—yes, full autonomy? Allowing each other to act and move and speak and create and love without challenging each other's actions? Without seeing them as threats or vices or signs that something is wrong with the world? For this is all that you do now.

Imagine, for a moment, that none of you attempted to invade each other's authority. You would, at first, feel elated, and then you would begin to move in the slightest way and begin to feel a tug and pinch, here and there, as you realized that you were all connected, as you realized that the binds and ties and links between you are not severable. You cannot sever them. You realize that autonomy is something you also co-create. But imagine, for a moment, that you were to view each other as moving without attempting to sever the links *and* without attempting to drag each other in one direction or another, to control the chains? How would you operate? What if you were to each say, *I will always operate to allow the other to move as autonomously as possible*? If you were to give each other that gift? Spend some time playing with this gift of autonomy for each of you. Imbue your interactions with the spirit of autonomy, of allowance, and see what emerges. See where you begin to feel the tug of your interconnectedness, your interdependence, and then continue to imbue that with the spirit of autonomy.

❈

Your system has been showing its weaknesses, its points of fraying, where the pieces that hold together your social fabric are fraying and pulling apart, exposing their weaknesses, exposing the places where you don't look, the lies that you tell yourselves that keep the social fabric together. The selection of your latest Supreme Court justice is a key example. Many of you wish to know whether the story that the victim told was true, and if so, you could then decide once and for all who was right and who was wrong.[2]

But that is not the way forward, either. For you miss the whole point of this event, which was that the world looked and said that there is a person who feels victimized here, and you decided that her story would somehow dictate whether this person was elevated to the task of making some of the most important decisions that your country can make and agree to. And we ask you, why did that become the means by which you decided this outcome? Why did it become a decision based on the veracity of this story? You marshaled so many resources in your nation in an attempt to reach a decision, to decide whether that person, the judge, was to receive this position.

Were there not other factors? Were there not other criteria you could have used to decide this outcome? Yes, of course, but you all fell into this as a sign that one person must be right, and the other person wrong, or one person did something and the other person was harmed, and this is the criteria by which you decided that this person was to assume this role of power. And you do so because you believe that this provides an objective measure of what you really want to say, which is that you have already made a decision, internally. *I want this* or *I do not want this. I like this* or *I do not like this.* And the reason is whether it serves you. Yes, you ultimately decide based on whether it serves you and you alone in some manner.

That is the ultimate decision-making process, and so these other means by which you reach collective decisions are mere subterfuges, they are farces, masking the internal decision-making that simply elevated the question of "does this serve me?" to something else, to something that seems more nuanced, that seems more elevated. And we wish for you to stop looking at the world and asking, *How does this serve me?* For that is the real question underlying most of your decisions and most of your reactions and judgment. And when you ask this question, *How does this serve me?*, you will recognize the ways in which you make the world a reflection of your own internal needs, trying to bend and shape the world around you.

What is the way out?

We have just shown you. The way out is to allow everyone an amount of autonomy. Everyone. And you say in response, *But others aren't going to respect my autonomy.* And so you have what you like to a call a *first-mover* or *collective action* problem, which is that someone else is always going to take advantage. And so no one wants to commit. And again, we say to you, that the very idea here is driven by this underlying question, *How does this serve me?*

The word that Patrick wants to interject is *sacrifice*. Let's explore the nature of sacrifice for a moment. Sacrifice is the idea of giving up the self, the idea of giving up one's own needs, and yet it comes with this idea of being taken advantage of, of having others ignore one's own autonomy and needs. A sense of being devoured by the others. And we ask you: Do you know that this is sacrifice? Do you know what the outcome is when you sacrifice your own needs by not making them the center point of how you look at and evaluate the world?

No, you do not. You do not know that this is like. For none of you actually sacrifices the self. You prostrate yourself and say, *Look at me, I'm giving myself to you.* Can you see how this illusion of sacrifice actually betrays the same question, *How does this serve me?* So that you can be seen and admired as someone who sacrificed themselves for the rest of the world, for the greater good. You do not know what this is like. And Patrick wants to offer the image of Martin Luther King, Jr., as someone who sacrificed himself, and we would say he is an example of someone who was willing to put his life on the line, face tremendous resistance and opprobrium, and then ultimately give his life in service to a greater ideal. Was there ego involved? Of course, as there always is, even among those of you who claim to be self-realized. The ego is a necessary part of operating in this continuum, in this plane, with space and time.

But that does not mean that there was not sacrifice, either. For ultimately, the question, *How does this serve me?* did not guide Martin Luther King, Jr.'s inquiry. It wasn't his guiding question. But for the vast majority of the souls on the planet, this your question.

And you find that it is not easy for you to imagine, just saying, *Well, I'll ask a different question.* And the underlying question then becomes, *How does* not *asking, 'How does this serve me' still serve me?* And there's this underlying desire to take on this amazing role as someone who transforms society, who becomes a figure beloved like Martin Luther King, Jr., and that is what also drives you: the desire to be adored and loved. This is what fuels your current effort to be seen constantly through all sorts of images. Your technology allows you to be seen and consumed, much like your Hollywood stars are, and you hope to be found and become famous. Again, driven by the desire to be loved and adored by many.

And the underlying question still is *How does this serve me?*

To abandon the question, you have to take actions that have nothing to do with you, but assure the needs of others, assure their autonomy, in ways that have nothing to do with your needs at all. And you will soon see how hard this is, for you immediately ask, *But what about my needs, like food and shelter?* And we do not say that these are inconsequential, that you have no such needs, only that you asking the question betrays the fact that the underlying concern is still, *How does this serve me, even a little bit, so I might survive?*

And we say that the only way forward is to embrace your status as a Seed of Light, to invoke the consciousness of the Christ, even as you ask that question, by saying, *I am the Christ, I am the Light, in and through the needs of others.* Can you invoke this as you go about your business? You cannot hide and wait for your mind to be cleared before doing and taking action. No, you cannot wait as if you were preparing yourself, becoming self-actualized, and then deciding, okay, now I can go out in the world. You must move forward, continuing to invoke your true nature even as you become deeply aware of how many of your actions are not driven by sacrifice but by your own need for security and safety.

And as you become aware of how much this question, *How does this serve me?*, guides your every thought and action, then you can begin to peel it away, slowly, over time. And you will soon see how much of your life has been and continues to be guided by it. That is the way forward to your emancipation. You cannot hole up and wait for this change to occur. You can only transform yourself in and through your relationships, your interactions with the world, for there is where you see how many of your actions are guided by this question, and how little autonomy you actually afford others.

※

Much has changed in the time since we last transmitted to you, for your society is undergoing massive disruption. As a society, you ask, *Where is this going? Are we actually improving? Are we simply heading towards disaster? Are we falling apart?* And we wish to ask you to pause and see that those are not the same thing. They are not in opposition. You are not necessarily falling apart *or* improving. In fact, it may be both—you may be falling apart and improving at the same time. Falling apart and improving are not to be seen in opposition. This is your binary mind wanting to see two divergent possibilities as an interpretation for the events that you are facing.

And instead of responding to them as if you had to choose between them, you might begin to suspend that very binary. Ask yourself, *How do I relate to what is occurring? How do I relate to it now?* You think that answering that question, *Am I falling apart or am I improving?*, determines how to respond to it. We wish for you to understand that this is not the case. It is not the case that you need the answer to whether you are falling apart or whether you are improving, to actually wake up and respond from the perspective of the Christ Consciousness, from the perspective of complete unity with what is occurring.

The answer is: It does not matter. That interpretation will point you to ways to respond that have nothing to do with what is actually occurring, and so you can suspend that way of looking at the world that says we are falling apart or we're improving, in order to find a response that is actually adequate to the situation.

Your response is always to be one of love. It is always love. You may be thinking that if the answer is, *Well, if we're falling apart, then we're going to need to fix things, we're going to take care of things, we're going to need to tell people you're doing this wrong, and this is what we need to be doing differently.* And if you think if you're improving, then your response is going to be, *Wonderful, this is improving, we're going to continue to do the same.* In other words, you think that the outcome is to do something different or to do the same, based on your perception of whether the situation is improving or not. And therefore you are going to take actions in response that are in fact the path that led you to that situation where you are now.

Elaborate, please.

What we mean to say is that by responding to the question you've imposed—*Are we falling apart or are we improving?*—you have determined that there are courses of action that you would take. Those courses of action that you would take are, in truth, the same ones that have led you to the situation where you are now, and neither is adequate. If you respond to a situation that you perceive to be damaging, threatening, and say, *We are falling apart, losing coherence, heading towards destruction*, you will respond with an attempt to fix that situation. Those are the ways you have responded already, in an attempt to protect the self from a world that you see is threatening, so you will behave in particular ways that have led you to the same outcome where you are now. If you think things are improving, you will continue to do things that you *think* led to the situation, that are going to improve your lives, and that are also a product from the same consciousness.

Can you give us a concrete example?

One example is the current administration, occupied by a person you call Donald J. Trump. And this person has behaved in ways that have defied the norms for how a President typically behaves; the ways in which he has behaved are in utter disregard of those norms. And some of you regard that as an improvement. Some of you look at that and say, *Look, he's changing the way it's done.* The people who support his actions will say, *This is an improvement. This is how we need to change the system.*

And those of you who regard his actions as causing damage and being perilous to society will say, *No, no, this is bad. This is bad. What we need to do instead is to remove him and return to the ways of old.*

Both of you then respond with actions that are based on the idea that what is occurring is a sign that things are *either* falling apart *or* improving. And one of the ways you will respond is to tell the other side, that sees this as the opposite view that you have, that they are wrong, and you will be in constant judgment of them. In other words, you will attempt to defend the system as it currently exists if you see it as improving, and those of you who see it as falling apart will attempt to defend the system that came before, the system that you see as being threatened.

How do we respond to the current situation?

We have explained that you must respond by injecting love and unity into the system, so that your actions themselves are infused with a particular intention. It is not your obligation to figure out whether you relate to it as falling apart or as improvement in order to determine a course of action. You're going to take a course of action; you're going to vote for someone to replace him or vote for him again. What we say to you is that you will inevitably make a decision. But it is more important that you *not* make a decision based on the view that what is happening now is a problem and needs to be improved upon, or what is happening now is an improvement and needs to be protected, which is the position you have all taken, which is the position you took when one set of you voted for him and another set voted against him. And therefore, you have led yourself to this situation, both sides acting in opposition, from a place of separation and in view of the idea that the world is either falling apart or improving.

You are both relating to it from a place of fear. You need to suspend this relationship of fear to what you are seeing before you, and not decide whether this right or wrong, falling apart or an improvement. Instead, relate to it with the desire for there to be unity among all of you, not for one side to lose and the other side to win. See yourself injecting a certain amount of energy into a system that will then shift and transform without you necessarily needing to answer this question of whether it is right or wrong. Imagine if you were to vote for somebody not because you were voting out of fear, but as an opportunity to express your unity with all people, and to say, *May this vote bring us all into unity.* If your every engagement with every person around these topics was, *How about do I relate to this person from a state of unity?*, your words and actions would be completely different.

We do not then tell you *this is what you must say and do*, because in turn you will simply replicate this as a formula, with something that allows you to then say, *I now know that I'm doing this right.* But therein lies the binary, once again: *Am I doing this right?* You would not be relating to this choice from a place of unity. You know what it means to operate from a place of fear, what it means to operate from a place of unity, to be in love and not be in opposition with somebody, to be connected with somebody in which your needs and their needs are not separate.

Those of you who have children know this very well. Those of you who have spouses may have experiences. And many of you have experiences of unity in other contexts. That is where you must go. That is the work ahead of you. It simply means repeating the formula, *I am the Christ as I do this* _____. *I am in unity as I do this* _____. It is the energy of your intention that you must interject into the system. Therefore, as you approach the next step of your evolution, and the evolution of your political system in which you face the question, *Do we re-elect this person or do we elect somebody else?*, you are going to be making decisions along the way. With each decision, it is important that, rather than deciding that this person is right or this person is wrong, you regard each of your choices as bringing unity. Ask yourself, *Will this person bring unity?*

You may not necessarily know the answer to that question, but it is the intention with which you enter this sphere that matters the most.

ACKNOWLEDGMENTS

T *his book is the third* installment of a series of channeled works that I downloaded in 2016. It has been waiting patiently in the wings for its debut while its other siblings enjoyed their time on stage. Perhaps because it had to wait or perhaps because of its subject matter, it feels like the most mature of them, despite being the youngest.

This book also marks a turning point in my own life, where I have embraced the role of being a conscious channel. It has not been an easy decision to let go of my previous life as a lawyer. Although many people in the spiritual world aspire to all sorts of psychic faculties and healing abilities, I have always felt a certain amount of reluctance in this arena. It is not because channeling doesn't feel real or that I don't enjoy it. To the contrary, it's one of the most amazing and blissful experiences I have ever had. But it has meant letting go of a very stable and conventional life as a lawyer, and witnessing the departures of cherished friends who could not understand this turn in my life. To be a channel is to assume a life path that draws a lot of skepticism, if not outright charges of mental illness. Few can understand the demands of this path until they have actually walked it themselves. To those of you who could not accompany me this far, thank you for being a part of my life for as long as you were. I am eternally grateful for the time that our lives were intertwined.

Nevertheless, the path has chosen me, as another gifted channel once said to me, and being true to myself has always been one of my most cherished values. I am trusting where this path will lead me. I do not know how it will unfold, but with the Council, I feel more guided and cared for than I ever did in the practice of law or as a professor of Spanish. I remain awed by this entire process, including the enormous blessings and healings that come each and every time I deepen my connection to this disembodied energy and wisdom.

Nor have I embarked on this path alone. I continue to be exceptionally grateful for all the incredible support I have received along the way. My teacher, Mirabai Devi, continues to be a guiding light in my life. Will McGreal remains one of my great supporters and most trusted confidants. Tony LeRoy has been a constant companion, witnessing my growth and gently and humorously offering advice. The love and support of my greatest champion, my husband, Max, is my touchstone every single day. And I have many friends and family members who have remained in my life, even if they don't fully understand who I am becoming.

To all of you, and many others who remain unnamed here, I could not have done this without you, and I love you more than words can adequately convey.

ABOUT THE AUTHOR

*P*atrick Paul Garlinger is an award-winning author and conscious channel. Nearly a decade ago, he experienced a profound spiritual awakening when he began to meet numerous spiritual teachers and experience higher states of consciousness. While completing his training under the renowned spiritual teacher, Mirabai Devi, Patrick underwent an awakening of his *kundalini* and channeled a series of works of spiritual wisdom between March and September 2016. The first volume, *Seeds of Light: Channeled Transmissions on the Christ Consciousness*, was published in March 2017 and awarded the 2018 Living Now Silver Medal for Metaphysics. *Bending Time: The Power to Live in the Now*, was released in June 2018. In addition, in 2016 Patrick published *When Thought Turns to Light: A Practical Guide to Spiritual Transformation*, a non-channeled introduction to spiritual techniques for readers seeking to incorporate more peace, joy, and wonder into their everyday lives, which won the 2017 Living Now Spirit Book Award.

Patrick lives in New York City, where he shares the wisdom he has learned with others so that they may know their own divine truth. For more information about his books and services, please visit www.patrickpaulgarlinger.com.

NOTES

INTRODUCTION

[1] For the Council, the phrase conveys that we are all divine, all connected to the Light, the source of all life, and that connection can never be taken away. Each of us is a "seed" of Light, one manifestation of the Light in physical form. Through the word "seed," they suggest that we are learning to grow our connection to the Divine and to shine brighter as we deepen that connection.

[2] In *Seeds of Light*, for example, the Council articulated its fundamental message about identity: "Understand that your claim to an identity is just a means of resisting the collective consciousness and its message of nonexistence and unworthiness . . . . It is not fully who you are. You are inherently limiting yourself in order to resist the limitation imposed by another" (160). Similarly, in *Bending Time*, the Council asserted: "[T]here is nothing wrong with categories of identity, insofar as they expand possibilities and allow you to see the expansion of ways of being human and living in a human body.... Identity becomes a shackle when it means you only allow certain experiences to exist and be visible" (64–65).

2. THE EGO AND THE TRUE SELF

[1] See "The Human Inclination to Judge," *Seeds of Light*, pp. 11–17, and "Seeing Each Other Anew," *Bending Time*, pp. 28–31.

6. RESPONSIBILITY FOR THE WHOLE

[1] As a reminder to the reader, on occasion I interject questions and comments in response to the Council's transmissions, which appear in the text offset in italics.

9. MASS INCARCERATION

[1] Forgiveness is a fundamental topic in *Seeds of Light*, as it is our power to rewrite the past. When we hold onto grievances, we're actually recreating the energy of the pain and suffering in the present moment, and forgiveness is our ability to reclaim our divinity, which is never wounded or harmed, and recreate ourselves in the present moment without the pain of the past. See "Forgiveness and the Christ Consciousness" and "Forgiveness is the Only Choice," *Seeds of Light*, pp. 128–30, 141–43.

10. ECONOMIC INEQUALITY

[1] *Bending Time* tackled the topic of money and asserted fundamentally that money is a form of energy transfer that we use to negotiate our separation from one another. It is nothing more than an agreement to exchange energy, in the forms of goods and services, between us. In that regard, money is a *creative* force that allows us to work with this material realm in the way that thoughts and language do not. For a more complete discussion, see "Memory as Creation," *Bending Time*, pp. 13–16.

11. SELF-INTEREST IN POLITICS

[1] See "On the Infinite Forms that Love Can Take," *Seeds of Light*, pp. 26–28, and "Our Relationship with Our Mothers," *Bending Time*, pp. 39–42.

12. MONEY AS SPEECH

[1] See "Memory as Creation," *Bending Time*, pp. 13–16.

13. CORRUPTION IN POLITICS

[1] The reader can consult *Seeds of Light* for the full discussion of what the Council means by that term.

14. DEMOCRATIC REPRESENTATION

[1] As the Council states in *Seeds of Light*: "Forgiveness is the mechanism of resurrecting yourself . . . because you are rewriting the past that you once had through the very act of forgiving . . . . You manifest a new reali-

ty that is not the same as you manifested the moment before you forgave" (pp. 131–32).

17. CORPORATE CONTROL OF FOOD

[1] See "Bending Time and Space," *Bending Time*, pp. 138–48.

[2] In *Seeds of Light*, the Council states that "[y]ou are mainly of the view that the world is to be compared against your own experience, against your own understanding of what it means to be human. You do this all other things you see, such as animals and plants. You compare them to humans and what they experience. You anthropomorphize. You talk about whether an animal speaks or has language or feels and has emotions, and if they relate to each other as families or not. You basically judge and evaluate against your template of being. Do plants and animals feel? Do they love? Do they dream? Yes, yes, and yes. But not in the ways that you think . . ." (8).

[3] In *Seeds of Light*, the Council explains that "nature has a consciousness, a way of connecting to all that is, and when you are in nature, you get a taste of it . . . . Nature already understands the nature of love, the function of love, the Creator's way of sending love, and you experience that lack of concern over love when you are in nature. Nature does not ask—who am I? Where do I belong? Why did this happen to me. No, the wind does not ask this, the trees do not ask this, the ground beneath your feet does not ask this. All of these know themselves as themselves, and they are in complete alignment with the love that comes their way. Not so you humans . . ." (10, 26–27).

20. POLITICAL PARTISANSHIP

[1] See "The Mind Is Structured Around Binaries" and "Binary Thinking Is Not Essential," *Seeds of Light*, pp. 38–41.

24. WHEN CHANGE HAPPENS

[1] The Council uses *agreement* in a novel way. It does not mean that you support or endorse whatever you are in agreement with. Rather, to be in agreement with something means that it is part of your reality, that you are aware of it. To *align* with something is to endorse it, support it, and hope for its manifestation. The Council's use of these terms in unfamiliar ways is part and parcel of their efforts to break our normal patterns of thought.

25. LIBERTY AND NEW POSSIBILITIES

[1] See "The Limits of Identity" and "The Fear of the Unknown," *Bending Time*, pp. 64–73. Much of *Bending Time* is devoted to the idea that we constantly replicate ourselves in a version of the past, something we already know, to avoid the fear and discomfort that come from not knowing what the future may bring. As a result, we often limit our possibilities only to those we already know or can anticipate, out of a profound fear of pain and, ultimately, death.

26. RELATING DIFFERENTLY TO THE WORLD

[1] See "On the Infinite Forms that Love Can Take," *Seeds of Light*, pp. 26–28, and "Releasing Expectation," *Bending Time*, pp. 126–36.

29. SEEING UNITY IN THE WORLD

[1] See "The Limits of Identity" and "Releasing Expectation," *Bending Time*, pp. 64–69, 126–36.

30. THE NEED FOR REPARATIONS

[1] See "Karma and Resurrection," *Seeds of Light*, pp. 69–76. I understand the Council here to be saying that the burden of overcoming structural racism cannot be placed at the feet of individuals by asking each black person to deal with the weight of racism individually.

[2] See "How Change Occurs," *Seeds of Light*, pp. 92–95.

[3] See "Forgiveness and the Christ Consciousness" and "Crucifixion as the Ego, Forgiveness as Resurrection," *Seeds of Light*, pp. 131–37.

32. THE TASK OF UNITING HUMANITY

[1] See "The Experience of Death," *Bending Time*, pp. 60–63.

CODA

[1] This portion was channeled in January 2019, as I was preparing the manuscript for publication.

[2] The Council is alluding to the events surrounding the confirmation of Justice Brett Kavanaugh and the allegations of abuse brought forth by Dr. Christine Blasey Ford.